Laying Foundations

Phase II

Knowing God

Pocket Principles®
and Guided Discussions

For Leaders

Knowing God, Pocket Principles® and Guided Discussions, For Leaders

For copyright information:
Worldwide Discipleship Association
(Attention: Margaret Garner)
P.O. Box 142437
Fayetteville, GA 30214 USA
E-mail: mgarner@disciplebuilding.org
Web Site: www.disciplebuilding.org

NOTE: In an effort to recognize that both men and women are co-heirs of God's grace, we have chosen to use alternating gender pronouns in this document. However, we do recognize and embrace gender-specific roles in Scripture.

Development Team:
Bob Dukes
Margaret Garner
Jack Larson
Margo Theivagt

Writing Team:
Bob Dukes
Margaret Garner
Jack Larson
Jon Long
Jeff Mares
Frank Mashburn
Margo Theivagt

Publishing Team:
Nila Duffitt
Buddy Eades
Margaret Garner
David Parfitt

Design by Cristina van de Hoeve · *doodlingdesigner.com*

A Welcome from WDA's President

Worldwide Discipleship Association, Inc.

Hello Friend!

Let me congratulate you on your decision to learn more about Jesus Christ and what it means to follow Him. There is nothing more important or more rewarding than the decision to follow Him and then to grow as a Christian.

These studies will help you get started on your journey with Christ or encourage and instruct you if you are already on this exciting journey. We in WDA want to help you grow and become all you can be in Christ Jesus!

Because you have chosen to lead, we want to do all we can to support you. In addition to the materials provided in this workbook, we would like to also offer you a free download of the Teaching Outlines for *Knowing God*.
www.disciplebuilding.org/materials/
knowing-god-teaching-outlines-free-download

My prayer and confident belief is that "he who began a good work in you will carry it on to completion until the day of Christ Jesus" (Philippians 1:6) so that He is able "to present you before his glorious presence without fault and with great joy." (Jude 1:24) To Him be glory and praise!

May God richly bless you as you strive to grow in Him.

Bob Dukes
President, Worldwide Discipleship Association
Fayetteville, GA 30214

Knowing God
Table of Contents: Leader

Leader's Instructions
For Using Pocket Principles®

What is a Pocket Principle™? Each Pocket Principle™ is a brief essay that focuses on a single topic necessary to the growth and maturity of a believer.

The 10 Pocket Principles®, about *Knowing God*, focus on enabling a new believer (or a mature believer who wants a fresh look at foundational truths) to begin getting to know God by spending time with Him, reviewing key concepts about Him (Who is the Trinity? God the Son? Holy Spirit? etc.) and learning about God's attributes and character.

Using Pocket Principles® in a Guided Discussion (small group) format:

You will notice that each Pocket Principle™ has a corresponding Guided Discussion. Because the students who are studying *Knowing God* are usually less mature believers, our suggestion is that they **not be required** to read the Pocket Principles® before coming to the Guided Discussion or after the Discussion. At this point in their maturity, it is best that they be given no work to do outside of the group discussion. (For more information about this, go to our website at www.disciplebuilding.org/about/phases-of-christian-growth/2.) Of course, you can mention the purpose of the Pocket Principles® and **invite** students to read them. The content of the Pocket Principles® will reinforce truth learned in the group discussion. Also, if a group member misses a meeting, he can read the corresponding Pocket Principle™ to review the information missed.

Using Bible Readings:

The booklet in this series entitled *Bible Readings for Devotional Use* is for the student to use in his devotional time. (The first lesson, *Relating To God*, focuses on having a devotional time.) The Bible readings (for a year) focus on the books of *John, Colossians, I John, Genesis, Exodus, Philippians, Jonah* and some of the *Psalms*. These books have been chosen because they emphasize many of the topics studied in the Cornerstone series. Please emphasize this to your students. The booklet contains instructions about how to use the readings. (The Exhibit after Lesson #1 contains only the instructions. For the passages etc., refer to the booklet *Bible Readings for Devotional Use*.)

Using Pocket Principles® in a Life Coaching (one-one) format:

Pocket Principles® can also be used effectively in an interactive one-one relationship. However, in this arrangement we suggest that the Life Coach (discipler) ask the student to read the Pocket Principle™ beforehand so the material can be discussed during a one-one appointment. All the dynamics mentioned above still apply, and the Life Coach needs to tailor expectations to the maturity of the student. To facilitate interaction, the material contained in the corresponding Guided Discussion-Leaders Edition will help a Life Coach prepare for the appointment. (For more information about preparing for a Life Coaching appointment, please consult the *Life Coaching Manual* at www.disciplebuilding.org/product-category/life-coaching.)

Leader's Instructions
For Using Guided Discussions

The 10 Guided Discussions, about *Knowing God,* focus on enabling a new believer (or a mature believer who wants a fresh look at foundational truths) to begin getting to know God by spending time with Him, reviewing key concepts about Him (Who is the Trinity? God the Son? Holy Spirit? etc.) and learning about God's attributes and character.

Guided Discussions for small groups play an important role in the growth of a believer with the **major goal being interaction around Scripture.** The goal of disciple building is not just knowledge, but Christlikeness in character and conduct. Therefore, **application is essential.** (Sections "Looking At Real Life" and "Looking at My Life" are application oriented.) At least one-third of the small group discussion time should be spent discussing application of the truth. It is often tempting to get caught up in the content part of the study, but you, as the leader, are responsible to move the group along to application.

A word needs to be said about the relationship between Pocket Principles® and Guided Discussions. The content of both is generally the same, although not identical. These 2 formats provide different ways of presenting the same content, or both can be used to reinforce the content. (Another type of WDA material is Teaching Outlines. These are designed to be used by a teacher who wants to present the content in a lecture format to a larger group. Free Teaching Outlines can be found at the WDA store on our website at www.disciplebuilding.org/materials/knowing-god-teaching-outlines-free-download.)

There are two (2) versions of each study: the Leader's version with answers and special notes, and the Student version with questions, but no answers. *Answers and notes to leaders are in gray, italicized text.*

Much of the preparation has been done for you as a leader: topics have been chosen, Scriptures chosen, questions written. However, it is important that you become comfortable with the material so that you will be able to be flexible and focus on the needs of your group. In the *Small Groups Manual* (WDA), you will find information about the practical aspects of group leadership. Please refer to the section titled "Practical Dynamics of Small Group Leadership." This is available from the WDA store at www.disciplebuilding.org/store/leadership-manuals/small-groups-manual.

Relating To God

You have begun a journey to know God, but did you know that you are actually joining a story in progress? God has desired to have a relationship with you for a long time and has prepared the way for you to enter into that relationship. When a person comes to faith in Christ and passes from spiritual death to life, a transaction takes place that has many far-reaching implications. One of these is complete and full reconciliation with God and the start of a new relationship. It is a relationship that is fuller, deeper, and richer than anything we can possibly imagine.

There are fundamental differences between God and mankind that impact the relationship and make it unlike human relationships. For example, God is infinite, while we are finite. He is all-knowing, while we have very limited understanding, both of the world we live in and the people around us. God is the Creator; we are created beings. He is invisible; we are visible. He is unchangeable; we change. God is perfect; we obviously are not.

However, there are also ways in which a relationship with God has many things in common with other relationships in our lives. That is, it requires time, conversation, mutuality, intimacy, etc. The best relationships are the ones in which we share at deep levels, consistently over a long period of time. Our relationship with God works the same way.

As with most relationships, our relationship with God is reciprocal. There are certain things that God does to establish and maintain the relationship, and there are specific things we must do for the relationship to grow and develop. Understanding this reciprocal dynamic and how it affects the relationship is very important. We can cultivate our relationship with God by understanding this reciprocal dynamic and by understanding how to nurture this relationship.

We also have a responsibility to obey the commands of God. This is love in action; love with shoes on.

GOD TAKES THE INITIATIVE IN HIS RELATIONSHIP WITH US.

He knows us intimately (Psalm 139:1-4).

God knows everything about us—our actions, our movements, our thoughts, our words. In fact, because He is all-knowing and exists outside of space and time, He knows these things before they even happen. He knows us far better than we know ourselves. Knowledge can be scary in human relationships. We choose what we think is safe to disclose to one another, and we go to great lengths to protect information we don't want others to know. We are free to be totally open and honest with God because He knows all about us anyway. And the amazing thing is that He loves us unconditionally despite full knowledge of everything about us that is unlovely.

He protects and shields us. He is our security (Psalm 139:5-6).

"You hem me in, behind and before," writes the psalmist. "You have laid your hand upon me." The laying of God's hand upon us is a picture of his all-encompassing care for us. In other Psalms, David uses many pictures to describe God's care of him including that of a shield, a fortress, a hiding place, a refuge, and a shelter. He paints the following picture in the first two verses of Psalm 91: "He who dwells in the shelter of the Most High will rest in the shadow of the Almighty. I will say of the Lord, 'He is my refuge and my fortress, my God, in whom I trust.' "

He is completely attentive to us regardless of our circumstances (Psalm 139:7-12).

"Where can I go from your Spirit?" wonders the psalmist. "Where can I flee from your presence?" He then reflects that no matter where he could possibly go, he knew that he could never go beyond the reach of God's personal concern.

> Part of the struggle and the joy of our lives comes from learning to persevere in habits of prayer.

This is a significant distinction between our relationship with God and that with any other person. No human, no matter how much he or she may want to, can ever always be there for us, either physically or emotionally. At some point, distance or other factors will prevent it. However, we can never go anywhere that God will not be with us.

He initiated and sustains our being: external (physical) and internal (emotional, spiritual) (Psalm 139:13-16).

One of the things we most value about those we are close to is that there is a strong bond of understanding between us. These special friends seem to understand what really makes us tick. Who knows better what makes a clock tick than the craftsman who builds the clock? Likewise, who knows us better than the God who created us? He knows us inside and out, better than anyone else ever can. He created us in His image to reflect His glory, yet He has created each of us uniquely with a predetermined number of days that we shall live upon this earth.

WE HAVE A RESPONSIBILITY IN OUR RELATIONSHIP WITH GOD.

To seek Him (Jeremiah 29:10-14)

"You will seek me and find me when you seek me with all your heart," was God's word to the Jews living in captivity (Jeremiah 29:10-14). The heart represents the center of one's being, the seat of emotions and will. Scripture includes several commands that relate to the heart: We are told to love God with all of our hearts (Deuteronomy 6:5 and elsewhere), to trust with all of our hearts (Proverbs 3:5), and to repent with all of our hearts (Joel 2:12).

Our seeking is not to be a casual endeavor. Consider the contrast between two men who go on separate camping trips. The first man realizes during the week that he has misplaced his pocketknife. It was a good knife, although relatively inexpensive. He would like to find it, and every day he keeps his eyes open for it in case he should happen to stumble across it.

Unlike other books, God's Word is living and spiritual, practical and dynamic.

The second man realizes the night before he is to leave to return home that he has lost his car keys. Early the next morning, he receives a call from his wife saying that their teenage son has been in a car accident and is in intensive care in the hospital. There is no casual searching here. He has got to find those keys! He scrambles around on his hands and knees, tears his tent and camping gear apart, and frantically retraces every step he made the previous day. The first man's search for his knife is a half-hearted effort; the second man's search for his keys is with his whole heart.

To love Him with our heart, soul and mind (Matthew 22:36-39)

A teacher of the law asked Jesus, "Of all the things we're expected to do, what is the most important?" Jesus replied, "Love the Lord your God with all your heart and with all your soul and with all your mind." (Matthew 22:37) According to the response that Jesus gave to the teacher, everything taught in the law can be summed up in this one commandment.

We have a responsibility not simply to acknowledge God's existence or even to acknowledge His rights as creator, but to love Him with our hearts, our souls, and our minds. This is another way of saying that we should love Him with every part of our being.

To obey Him (John 14:21)

We also have a responsibility to obey the commands of God. This is love in action; love with shoes on. According to the words of Jesus, obedience is how we show our love for God (John 14:21). The Apostle John, who recorded these words, later reiterates Jesus' words by stating flatly, "This is love for God: to obey His commands." (I John 5:3) John also argues that if we say we have come to know God (have a relationship with Him) yet do not obey His commands, then we are lying (I John 2:4).

To draw near to Him (James 4:8)

James, the brother of Jesus, writes, "Come near to God and He will come near to you. Wash your hands, you sinners, and purify your hearts, you double-minded." (James 4:8) This verse speaks of another responsibility we have in our relationship with God. It also speaks of our outward actions (wash your hands) and our inward thoughts and motives (purify your hearts). Each is important as we draw near to God. Because we are sinful beings, we will continue to do things that create distance in our relationship with God. Each time we become aware of this distance, we should once more humble ourselves, confess our sin and draw close to God. We draw near in need; He draws near in fullness.

...the amazing thing is that God loves us unconditionally despite full knowledge of all about us that is unlovely.

Notice that each of the responsibilities discussed above comes with a promise—a positive benefit for us as we fulfill the responsibility. This pattern further illustrates the reciprocal nature of our relationship. When we seek God, He allows Himself to be found by us, and He reveals His gracious plans for us. When we demonstrate our love by obeying God, He shows His love to us and reveals Himself to us. When we draw near to God, He draws near to us.

OUR RELATIONSHIP WITH GOD IS NURTURED BY INTERACTING WITH HIM.

Every good relationship thrives on shared experiences and a true knowledge of each other. In its essence, Christianity is a relationship between the people of God and the Living God. By revealing Himself to us and reconciling us to Himself through Jesus Christ, God sought us out and began this relationship. In response, we are to actively pursue God and cultivate our relationship with Him. We can do this by spending time with Him.

But people often ask, "How do you spend time with God when you can't see Him?" Fortunately, God has shown us how. He's given us His Word——the

4

Bible—and He meets with us in prayer. As we consistently read the Bible and pray to God, we grow closer to Him. As we see how He interacts with people in the Bible, we come to understand His character, His values, and His personality. Through our time in His Word and prayer, God embraces us and transforms our lives.

We interact with God through the Word.

Reading and contemplating the Bible can be a powerful experience. Unlike other books, God's Word is living and spiritual, practical and dynamic. Consider this: God, our Living Creator, has spoken! He has begun a dialogue with us, revealing His infinite thoughts to our finite minds through the Bible.

In its essence, Christianity is a relationship between the people of God and the Living God.

The Book of Hebrews says God's Word is living and active (4:12). Through it, God engages our whole being—soul, spirit, body, mind and heart. As we read and obey His Word, it has a profound influence in our lives. Psalm 19:7-14 tells us that God's Word is able to revive our souls, make us wise, encourage us, and guide us. More than just good advice, God's Word is a significant part of His conversation with His people.

Spending time with God's Word is like having an audience with a king. This means we must approach the Bible as we would approach God Himself: humbly and obediently. Jesus told His followers, "Whoever has my commands and obeys them, he is the one who loves me. He who loves me will be loved by my Father, and I too will love him and show myself to him." (John 14:21) Spending time with God's Word is not simply an exercise in scholarship or self-improvement but a faithful expression of our reverence and love for God Himself. With a teachable attitude and a willingness to be changed, we come closer to God through His Word.

God's Word is just that—His Word. As such, it bears the full integrity of His character and the limitless strength of His sovereignty. In Psalm 37, David tells us that God will accomplish what He promises. He also exhorts us: "Delight yourself in the Lord and He will give you the desires of your heart." (verse 4) Therefore, we ought to look to the Bible with expectant hearts and minds, eager to see God reveal His truth and accomplish His will among us. Do you expect God to reveal Himself to you in His Word? Does loving obedience result from your time with God in His Word?

We interact with God through prayer—having a conversation with Him.

Unlike our earthly friendships, our communion with God doesn't have to have interruptions. Our lives can truly be an unending dialogue with the Lord. Praying to God continues our conversation with Him, building upon the time we spend with God in His Word.

But what is prayer? Prayer, the Apostle John writes, is our response to God's outreach to us. The Lord says, "Here I am! I stand at the door and knock. If anyone hears my voice and opens the door, I will come in and eat with him, and he with me." (Revelation 3:20) Prayer is a yielding to God and an acceptance of His fellowship, as simple as a word of welcome or a cry for help.

> More than just good advice, God's Word is a significant part of His conversation with His people.

Nevertheless, a life of prayerful attention to God doesn't always come easily. Part of the struggle and the joy of our lives comes from learning to persevere in habits of prayer. God, in His grace, teaches us to pray and gives many examples of prayer in the Bible. For example, Psalm 25 shows some of the roles prayer can have in our lives. Prayer can be a way of entrusting yourself to God, expressing your hope in Him, seeking guidance, asking forgiveness, gaining His perspective, seeking refuge and receiving His comfort.

We also see elements of prayer in other Psalms. Psalm 100 is a brief expression of *thanksgiving*, calling us to worship the Lord with gladness and joyful songs, to acknowledge Him as our creator and leader, to praise Him for His enduring love and faithfulness. Psalm 51, David's song of contrition and hope, is also a model of faithful prayer. He *confesses* his sin and pleads for mercy (verses 1-9). Seeking God's help, he entrusts himself to His goodness and sustaining power (*petition*) (verses 10-15). He seeks the establishment of God's Kingdom and asks God to bless others (*intercession*) (verses 16-19).

At its simplest, faithful prayer is how we thank, praise and worship God. It requires no great programs or resources. As we have seen the Apostle James says, "Come near to God, and he will come near to you." (James 4:8a) This nearness of God is truly the essence of your relationship with Him. When you interact with God through His Word and in prayer, you're coming closer to God. By setting apart a time and place to devote your attention to God, you'll establish habits that will transform your relationship with Him.

SUMMARY

Christianity is essentially a relationship with God. By spending time with God in His Word and in prayer, we can grow closer to Him.

- Our relationship with Him is reciprocal. He initiates; we respond. He wants us to pursue Him.

- God reveals His character, will and goodness through the Bible.

- We should approach God's Word with gratitude, humility and obedience.

- God uses His Word to help us and change our lives.

- Prayer is our response to God beginning a conversation with us.

- The Bible gives many examples of the roles prayer can have in our lives.

- It helps to have specific times to meet with God in His Word and in prayer.

The booklet in this Cornerstone series called *Bible Readings for Devotional Use* provides 52 weeks of Bible readings from books of the Bible that cover topics emphasized in the lessons that follow. This booklet can be purchased in the WDA store at www.disciplebuilding.org/product-category/cornerstone. The Exhibit entitled *Bible Readings for Devotional Use (Instructions)* (which follows this lesson) is the instructions page of the booklet mentioned above. It will help orient you to spending time with God. It provides practical ideas about prayer and about Bible reading and Bible study.

Bible Readings For Devotional Use
Instructions

"God is most glorified when we are most enjoying Him."

The side quote from John Piper, Christian speaker and author, serves as an excellent introduction to the devotional life. The purpose of devotions is to know and enjoy God personally as you spend time with Him each day. James tells us, "Come near to God and He will come near to you."(4:8a) Two of the ways we draw near to God are in prayer as we listen and talk with Him and as we "hear" His voice in Scripture. (There are many aspects to drawing close to God, but only two will be discussed here.)

- **Praying** is conversing with God: listening and talking. Our conversation with God improves as we get to know Him, just as conversation with a friend becomes easier and more rewarding as the relationship grows. Some of the ingredients in prayer are:

  Thanksgiving, praise and worship—(Example in Psalm 100)

  Confession— (Example in Psalm 51:1-9)

  Committing myself to God— (Example in Psalm 51:13,15)

  Petition—making personal requests for self (Example in Psalm 51:10-12)

  Intercession— making requests for others (Example in Psalm 51:18)

- **Reading His Word** is a second aspect of drawing near to God. The goal, at this point in your walk with God, is not to do an in-depth study or to completely understand each idea/truth presented. In fact, no one, no matter how mature and educated, understands everything in God's Word because its depths are as unsearchable as He is.

The goal is to focus on what you do understand. As you grow, more and more of the truths in Scripture will become clear to you. It is much like putting a puzzle together. At first, individual pieces may be confusing or meaningless; however, as the pieces are joined together, they begin to reveal a picture that is meaningful. Although you may be unsure of some Scripture passages at first, your understanding will increase over time as you grow in your overall experience with Scripture. Do not become distracted or discouraged if you do not understand a specific passage. Instead, focus on what you do understand. Remember that the Holy Spirit is your teacher and "will guide you into all truth" at His pace. (Of course, if a question is particularly bothersome to you, talk with your mentor, small group leader or pastor.)

Some useful categories of questions to ask as you read a passage of Scripture are:

Observation questions: What are the facts?

Interpretation questions: What do they mean?

Application questions: How do they apply to me?

A word about versions of the Bible—there are many good versions of the Bible to choose from. We suggest that you use the New International Version. In our opinion, it is the most readable version and facilitates understanding. Of course, you are free to use any version that is recommended by your church or group.

Two principles of Scripture—

First—when reading and studying Scripture it is essential to understand the context in which a passage occurs. There are two different ways to use the word "context." "Context" may refer to the cultural setting. For example, knowing the "context" of your life (who your parents are, where you grew up, etc.) enables someone to understand you more fully. In a similar way, knowing the context of a passage of Scripture enables the reader to correctly understand the passage's meaning. The word "context" may also refer to the flow of thought in the text. For example, what happened immediately before? what was said? what happened afterwards? In Scripture, both usages of the word "context" are important.

Second—when seeking to understand Scripture, it is important to know the author's intent. The meaning is static: it means what the author originally intended it to mean. It does not change over time, from culture to culture, etc. Although there is only one meaning there may be many applications. For example, a truth from Scripture is, "Love your neighbor." There are many ways this truth can be applied. These ways vary according to the person, the circumstance, the amount of time available, etc.

Keeping a journal is a way to maximize the benefit from your times with God. We strongly suggest that you get a notebook and write down insights you have, things you learn about God, things you learn about yourself, sins you need to confess, things you are thankful for, etc. You might want to designate part of the journal as your "Prayer List," where you keep a list of prayer requests and answers!

A question that invariably arises is, "How long should my devotional time be?" There is no specific "right" length of time, just as there is no right amount of time for two good friends to spend together. If having a devotional time is new to you, begin with 15 or 20 minutes and increase as you are able.

A resource that might be quite helpful to you is a booklet published by InterVarsity Press entitled *Quiet Time: A Practical Guide for Daily Devotions.* This publication includes encouragement and practical suggestions and can be ordered through Christian bookstores or on the internet.

These instructions are from a booklet called *Bible Readings for Devotional Use* which can be purchased from the WDA store at www.disciplebuilding.org/store. The booklet will give you 52 weeks of Bible readings, as well as background and special notes about certain passages. The books of the Bible chosen are books that emphasize some of the principles focused on in the Cornerstone materials.

Exhibit

10

Relating To God

IMPORTANT to Leader: Answers and notes to leaders are in gray, italicized text. Much of this lesson will be you talking, instructing about having a Quiet Time and then demonstrating a QT. The remainder of these lessons will require less talking by you, and more by the students.

GOAL:

For a disciple to experience a devotional time with God during the small group session and commit to having a personal daily devotional time.

GETTING STARTED:

Think of the person you consider your "best friend." What are some elements that contributed to the development of this close relationship?

Responses will most likely be spending one-on-one time together, meaningful conversation, sharing about your struggles, etc.

Transition: In this lesson, we will learn how to use these same relational elements in relating to God and growing in our relationship with Him.

STUDYING TOGETHER:

To grow in a relationship with God there must be two-way (reciprocal) communication.

Read Psalm 139:1-16.

1. What do these verses say about God's relationship with us?

   He knows us intimately, He protects us, is our security, is completely attentive to us, initiates with us, sustains us.

2. Looking at the following verses: What are some of our responsibilities in our relationship with God?

   Jeremiah 29:10-14 *To seek Him*

   Matthew 22:36-39 *To love Him with heart, soul and mind*

   James 4:8 *To draw near to Him*

   John 14:21 *To obey Him*

We develop our relationship by spending time with God doing two very important activities.

First, we must learn to **Listen to God through His Word.**

As we read the Word, God may want to speak to us about any number of things. He may show us a sin to confess, a promise to claim, an attitude to change, a commitment to make, a praise to offer, something to thank Him for, a command to obey, an example to follow, a prayer to pray, an error to avoid, a truth to believe.

Second, we must learn to **Talk to God through Prayer.**

Prayer is essentially a conversation with God. In prayer, we can express praise and thanks; ask God for guidance; confess our sins; receive peace and comfort; commit ourselves to God; ask Him to meet our needs; ask Him to work in the lives of others.

Let's have a devotional time together as a group.

You will model what it means to have a devotional time with God during this study.

3. Open the devotional time in prayer.

Open the group devotional time with prayer asking God to give you wisdom as you read His Word.

4. Select a passage of scripture to read. (For our study today, we will read James 1:22-25 silently.)

Do not merely listen to the word, and so deceive yourselves. Do what it says. Anyone who listens to the word but does not do what it says is like a man who looks at his face in a mirror and, after looking at himself, goes away and immediately forgets what he looks like. But the man who looks intently into the perfect law that gives freedom, and continues to do this, not forgetting what he has heard, but doing it--he will be blessed in what he does. James 1:22-25

5. Take a few moments and write down some insights that especially spoke to you. You may also include an action step that God may want you to take. To start with, write no more than a paragraph.

Of course during a devotional time you will be alone and won't be sharing aloud with others, but in order to give the group an example to follow, you take the initiative and share your thoughts after giving the group a few minutes to write down their own thoughts. Or you may share the example provided below.

Example: God showed me that I am more interested in knowing what the Bible says rather than doing what it says. I know that if I'm going to change and grow in my walk with Him, I have to begin applying God's principles and promises to my life. I will begin asking God to show me how to apply His truth to my life when I have my daily devotional time with Him.

6. Next, spend some time praying to God in a conversational style as if He were sitting in a chair right in front of you.

Let the group watch and listen to you pray. Ask them to notice the different elements of prayer that are utilized. Use your own prayer or use the example provided below.

> *Example: Lord, I praise you because you are faithful to carry out the promises in your Word.*
>
> *I haven't been reading the Bible like I know I need to. Help me to be more consistent in studying your Word and applying it to my life.*
>
> *I pray that you would give me wisdom as I talk with my neighbor over dinner about what it means to know Christ. Give me the words to say. I pray that you would draw him into a relationship with Christ. I pray that the Holy Spirit would convict him of his sin and show him his need for a Savior.*
>
> *Lord, I also pray for my co-worker, that you would reconcile his marriage.*
>
> *And, I lift up to you my good friend, Jenny, that you would help her find a job. Give her peace and trust in you as she goes through this difficult time of unemployment.*
>
> *Lord, thank you for hearing my prayer. Help me to follow your Spirit's lead today and to glorify you in all I do. In Jesus' name, Amen.*

LOOKING AT REAL LIFE:

7. What benefits do you see to having a daily Quiet Time?

LOOKING AT MY LIFE:

There are three things involved in making a commitment to having a personal daily devotional time.

a. **Choose a Time**—The best time is often in the morning before the day begins. Make it a priority in your day.

   The time of day that works best for me is _____.

b. **Choose a Place**—The place should be quiet with no distractions where you can be alone.

   The place where I will have my devotional time is _____.

c. **Develop a Plan**—*If time allows, give group members the opportunity to read the accompanying Exhibit,* Bible Readings For Devotional Use (Instructions), *during the meeting. Otherwise, encourage them to read it on their own. After reading it, each person should be able to come up with a simple plan for a devotional time of 15 to 20 minutes. Be sure to remind them that it is better to set a small goal time-wise and be successful than to set a big goal and be frustrated.*

Leader:

Close the group in prayer asking God to give each person the discipline to have a personal devotional time each day. Ask group members to be ready at the next meeting to talk about their experiences during devotional times this week.

About Prayer: Since this series of studies is directed toward young believers, we are suggesting that their involvement in group prayer be progressive: from listening to the teacher pray, to participation using simple sentence prayers and on to spontaneous praying. Often young believers have little or no experience with public prayer and may be hesitant to pray aloud. Using a progressive approach will help them become comfortable praying aloud. Be sensitive about where group members are in their development and involve them accordingly. If group members are more mature Christians, of course you may let them participate in the prayer. Tailor the prayer to the maturity and needs of the group.

God Reveals Himself

One of the most wonderful things about God is that He wants everyone to know Him. Everyone! But there are many people in the world (over 6 billion), and most of them live in places where there is limited or no access to the Bible. Does that mean that most of these people can never know anything about God?

The answer to this important question is "No." In our relationship with God He initiates towards us by revealing Himself to us. If He didn't do this, we would be severely limited in our ability to know anything about Him. If we were on our own trying to understand God, our conclusions would be distorted, and there are things about Him we would never know.

Just how has God revealed Himself to us? His most obvious revelation is in His Word, the Bible. The Bible is one type of what we call special revelation: God's particular communications and manifestations of Himself to particular people at particular times. But what about people who have no access to the Bible? God has chosen to communicate with them in another way: natural revelation. Natural revelation is God's communication of Himself to all persons at all times and in all places; revelation that is generally available to all people. Let's look at natural revelation first.

NATURAL REVELATION

External Witness: Creation

Creation itself is revealing something to people about God.

How do we know that God communicates to people through natural revelation? If you didn't have a Bible, could you know that God is trying to tell you something? In all of history we see mankind preoccupied with questions about whether God or gods exist, and if so, what He or they are like. Where do people get these questions? Why does the subject come up in practically every culture in all of history? The answer is that the human situation forces these questions to arise. The world is made in such a way that it provokes the questions. In other words, the creation itself is revealing something to people about God.

Another way we know that God reveals Himself through nature is that the Bible tells us that He does. Romans 1:19-20 and Psalm 19:1-6 affirm that God is revealed through what has been created by Him. The Romans passage tells us that people know that there is a God because of what He has made. Perhaps Paul, the author of Romans, had in mind the following observations: Just as a watch needs a watch-maker, a house needs a house-maker, and a computer needs a computer-maker, the complexities and order of the universe point toward a universe-Maker. This Maker must not Himself be created, because then He would need a Maker, too (and that Maker would need a Maker, and so on). So, some Force outside of creation must have been responsible for creation. You might be thinking, "All right; so nature points to some Force that has created it…but that doesn't necessarily point to the God of the Bible." That's true, but keep reading!

Creation doesn't only tell us that the complexity and order in the universe need a cause. The *wonder* and *beauty* of the natural world tell us that the cause is personal and good. Think of some of the most beautiful places you know of—the Grand Canyon, or an island in Hawaii, a sunset over the ocean, or a grand waterfall in the mountains. What do you feel when you experience scenes like these? You're searching for words, aren't you? Glorious, gorgeous, magnificent, proud, resplendent, or maybe superb? It's hard to find just the right words to portray the indescribable beauty that we sometimes encounter in nature, isn't it? This beauty points to a God that is imaginative, personal, beautiful, and artistic.

Internal Witness: Image of God in Mankind

Not only do we see evidence of God in nature around us, we also see it in ourselves! The Bible says in Genesis 1:26-27 that God made men and women in His image. (Think about that! God's image!) In other words, there is something about us that is somehow like God. But what?

The "image of God" in people has to do with the following things:

- **God is a thinking Being**…we are thinking beings. We both (God and us) think!

- **God is an emotional Being**…we are emotional beings. We both feel!

- **God is a Being that makes choices**…we are beings that make choices. We both choose!

- **God is a creative Being**…we are creative beings. We both make things!

- **God is a moral Being**…we are moral beings. We live in a universe where there is right and wrong.

Just because we are like God in some ways doesn't mean we are like Him in all ways. For instance, God always does what is right! We don't. And, God is an all-powerful Creator. But we are much more limited, aren't we?

The point about morality is especially important. The moral natures of all people point toward the image of God in mankind. All people, in all cultures, have a sense of right and wrong, although different cultures work this out somewhat differently. However, there are some standards of goodness that are the same everywhere. For example, can you imagine a culture where the idea of a friend was someone that you do terrible things to and try to destroy? Can you imagine a culture where most people think that it is good to torture babies merely for the pleasure of it?

In Romans 2:14-15 and 3:19-20 Paul talks about the moral law that is on the hearts of all people. This is a type of natural revelation. He is saying that, even without a Bible, people have a basic knowledge of right and wrong. They may be mixed up about it all, but they still have remnants of moral knowledge. This doesn't mean that people all think exactly the same about issues of right and wrong, but it does mean that people all *act* as though there *is* real right and wrong…and they know some things are right. They may say that they don't believe in right or wrong until you steal something from *them*, or hurt *them*, or lie to *them*! They may suppress this knowledge in unrighteousness, but they still have some knowledge of it through natural revelation.

If we didn't have an idea of something perfect, how would we ever know we are not perfect?

Another way to see natural revelation at work is to notice the instinctive need to worship that people have. All people in all civilizations worship something. Of course, you have your atheists, too, but even they are "worshipping" something (e.g., Themselves, Humanity, Careers, Money, etc.). We are creatures of vast needs, and we have an instinctive knowledge that we need more than we can provide for ourselves.

And, we also know that we're not what we "ought" to be. You've heard the saying, "Nobody's perfect"? That is a moral truth gleaned from natural revelation. We all have our frailties and imperfections…but what sense would it make to talk about imperfection if there was not an idea of a Perfect Being somewhere? If we didn't have an idea of something perfect, how would we ever know we were not perfect?

Summing up, we can appreciate the multitude of ways God reveals Himself to us through natural revelation, and thank Him for what He has shown us about Himself: that He is the Creator, He is powerful, He is personal, He is beautiful, and He is wise. But the revelation is limited. It doesn't tell us how to be right with Him. Somehow God has to tell us His thoughts and His plan about our imperfections and sins, and for that, and many other things, we must look at special revelation.

SPECIAL REVELATION

If we went through life only knowing what natural revelation could deliver, we wouldn't have answers for many important questions:

What is God like? Does He like me, or is He mad at me because of my sins? Is He going to destroy me?

Is He a God that I can know and with whom I can have a relationship? Can I talk to God? Can He hear me? Does God have a plan for me?

How should I live on this earth? Are some things really right or wrong? How should I relate to other people? What is the best way to live my life?

Is there life after death? If so, is it in heaven? Am I going there?

As you can see, these are crucial questions that are central to much of our lives. Although these questions cannot be answered through natural revelation, the good news is that God also reveals Himself through *special revelation*. We've defined special revelation as revelation given especially to a particular individual or group(s) at a particular time.

God reveals Himself through special revelation in two main ways: the Bible and specific revelation to individuals and/or communities. Let's take a look at these two categories in greater depth.

The Bible

The Bible is a very precious revelation from God. The origin of the Bible is God Himself (II Timothy 3:16). He used various human authors and inspired what they wrote, working through their personal gifts, styles and cultures. Although the Bible is available to many people it is called special revelation because it is not available universally to everyone in the same way that natural revelation is.

The types of things that the Bible can teach you are incredible. Some of the important truths you can learn from the Bible include:

- The character and nature of God—many things about who God is and what He is like (e.g. Psalm 103)

- God's existence as a Trinity—the Father, the Son, and the Holy Spirit

- Prophecies about key events—especially about the Messiah coming (e.g. Isaiah 53)

- Jesus as the Messiah and the Savior of the world

- The significance of Jesus' life, teachings, sacrificial death, resurrection, and His coming again

- How to live the Christian life

- How to know God's will

Of course, there is much, much more. An interesting thing about the Bible is that, it's alive! (See Hebrews 4:12.) As you read and study the Bible, you will find that it is "searching you," telling you things about yourself that you know are true. So, reading the Bible can be an encounter with the Holy Spirit as He reveals truth, uncovers sin, and brings you comfort. Think of it…an actual encounter with God!

One of the best things about the Bible is that it tells us about Jesus Christ. In the book of John it tells us that, in Jesus, God came and dwelt among us (John 1:1,14). In other words, if you want to know what God is like, look at Jesus (John 1:18). Jesus is the second Person of the Trinity in human form; He is the most full expression of God that finite human beings can understand (Colossians 1:15; Hebrews 1:1-4).

The Bible tells us more about Jesus' life and teachings than any other historical source. If you want to get to know who Jesus is, you need to spend a lot of time in the Bible, especially in the four Gospels.

Special Revelation to Individuals and/or Communities

However strange it may seem, you can read the Bible all day and not get much out of it. In order to understand Scripture, the Holy Spirit must take the truths of God's Word and reveal them to you (John 15:26, 16:13-14). This is part of God's special revelation. Not only does the Holy Spirit have a part in you genuinely understanding the Bible, so do you. You need to approach the Scriptures with a humble attitude (an openness to obey what God shows you) if you want Him to reveal Himself to you (John 14:21).

At times God reveals His will for us in ways other than the Holy Spirit working through the Word. One way the Bible mentions is dreams and visions. Of course, dreams and visions are not always (or even usually) from God; nonetheless, the Bible cites occasions where God revealed something to someone in a dream and/or vision. You can read about some of the most famous of these in: Genesis 37, Matthew 1:18-24, Acts 10 and Acts 16:9-10.

Another type of special revelation is miracles. Luke 11:14-20 is one place among many where a miracle is used by God to show something to people. Of course, this does not mean that people will always attribute the miracle to God. For example, some people in the Luke 11 passage said that Jesus' power was from the devil. Sadly, they missed the significance of the miracle: to show them that "the Kingdom of God has come to you." The Bible is unashamedly full of miracles. And of course, that makes sense…if the God of the Bible exists, then miracles are automatically possible.

Another type of special revelation can be called "promptings of the Holy Spirit." We see an example of this in Acts 16:6-7 and in John 10. It seems to describe how God talks to us at times through a kind of "inner voice," or "inner sense." Not only does the Holy Spirit do this, but the Bible also tells us that Jesus is always with us and that the Father's presence is continually close by, to be with us and guide us.

Jesus said in John 10 that His sheep hear His voice and follow Him. An important part of the Christian life is cultivating a relationship with God to the extent that you can recognize His voice when He is talking to you. God is alive, and He is personal (that is, He has emotions, will and rationality). He doesn't want us to just know about Him, He wants us to know Him. You can expect Him to give you personal insights, comfort, admonishment, and guidance.

Not only will God give individuals specific inner guidance, He at times will guide communities in a similar manner. In Acts 15 (the Jerusalem Council), the disciples who were the leaders of the Jerusalem church were guided by a "group-sensing," a community reception of God's will for them, when they were in a difficult situation.

At times you may find that God is guiding your church, your small group, your family, etc. in a similar way. Sometimes you will not know what to do individually, but you will find that God's will becomes clear through a group. This is a good reminder, once again, that God has made us in such a way that we need one another. He is not only concerned with how we are doing with Him, but also how we are doing with each other.

SUMMARY

God is such a good God—everybody ought to know Him! He has revealed Himself in natural and special revelation so that all people may know Him and His ways.

As you seek Him, remember how important it is to approach the Bible with humility and an obedient heart, and in community with other followers of Jesus. Also keep in mind how near God's actual presence is to you, and how you can experience Him relationally. And be aware of how God might be revealing Himself to you in the other ways that were mentioned. May God disclose Himself to you more and more. *"Then you will **know** the **truth**, and the **truth** will set you free." (John 8:32)*

God Reveals Himself

GOAL:

For a disciple to understand that God has initiated toward mankind by revealing Himself by means of natural and special revelation.

GETTING STARTED:

What can you know about a person just by observing him?

grooming, physical attributes like height, hair color, body build, etc., clothing, etc.

What can you know about a person only if he chooses to tell you about himself?

background info such as birthplace and date, parents and siblings names, childhood experiences, hopes and dreams for the future, likes and dislikes, hobbies, etc.

Transition: In much the same way, God has revealed Himself to us.

STUDYING TOGETHER:

We need to begin with a definition:

Natural Revelation: God's communication of Himself to all persons at all times and in all places; revelation generally available to all people.

Read Psalm 19:1-6 and Romans 1:19-20.

1. How do you see God revealed in creation?

   In nature, in nature's provision for our needs (food, sun, water, etc.) the order, complexity and intricacy of nature, beauty of nature, etc.

   Leader: Hopefully students will touch on ideas such as the order, complexity, etc. of nature and not just on the physical objects in creation such as the sun, sky, etc.

Read Genesis 1:26-27.

2. According to these verses, what is another way God has revealed himself to all of us?

   He made all of us in His image.

What does this mean?

We are like him in that we have an ability to reason, create, feel, make choices, rule, etc. We can understand something about God by looking at people.

Read Romans 2:14-15.

3. What do these verses say about the morality of all men?

   God has given everyone an internal sense of right and wrong (even if they don't have the "law" or a Bible).

4. Where can we see evidences of this morality, this internal sense of right and wrong in our world today?

   Even though behaviors vary from culture to culture, every culture has standards of "right and wrong" that they enforce. Even people who say they don't believe in right or wrong get upset if they think someone steals from them, or hurts them, or lies to them.

   Also, there are some standards of goodness that are the same everywhere. For example, it is doubtful that there is a culture where people believe that it is good to torture infants just for pleasure.

   Also, children have a strong sense of right and wrong from a very young age. This is obvious when one of their "rights" is denied to them (food, toys, etc.).

Natural revelation is important, but it is not enough to tell us everything we need to know about God, such as how we can have a relationship with Him. There is another kind of revelation.

Special Revelation: God's particular communications and manifestations of Himself to particular people at particular times. (It is what we know about God because He has told us about Himself.)

5. God has given us a book and a person. What is the book, and who is the person?

   The Bible and Jesus

Read II Timothy 3:15-17.

6. Where does the Bible come from and what is its purpose?

It comes from God (is "God-breathed"). Its purpose is to teach, rebuke, correct and train us in righteousness.

Read Hebrews 1:1-3. Jesus came to reveal the Father; so we would know what He is like.

7. According to these verses, what was unique about Jesus?

Jesus was the exact representation of God by which He made God known to us and provided our salvation.

Read Acts 16:6-7, 9-10.

8. What are other ways God reveals things to His people at special times and in particular circumstances?

Through the Holy Spirit (visions, miracles, promptings of the Spirit)

LOOKING AT REAL LIFE:

9. God has taken the initiative to reveal Himself to us through creation and through His Word and Jesus. How do you think we should respond to this initiative?

Awe, love, humility, joy, gratitude, obedience, loyalty

LOOKING AT MY LIFE:

Share one or two ideas that God has revealed to you through special revelation in the past few months. How did He reveal these ideas to you (prayer, Word, Holy Spirit)?

Leader: Pray a prayer of praise and thanksgiving for the ways God reveals Himself to us.

The Attributes Of God

A.W. Tozer, a revered Pastor of the last century, wrote, "What comes into our minds when we think about God is the most important thing about us."[1] He realized that how we think and feel about God affects how we relate to Him. And as Christians, our relationship with God should be the most important relationship in our lives. In order to think correct thoughts about God (which is taken up in Pocket Principle™ #4, *Correcting False Views of God*) we must first understand His attributes, His inherent characteristics.

Having said that, we must realize that we cannot know God perfectly. The finite cannot know everything about the infinite. In our attempts to describe God, to know Him, there is a natural temptation to limit Him; to try to make Him more like us and less than He truly is. We must fight this tendency and meditate on what He has revealed about Himself. We need a big picture of God if He is going to be worthy of our complete trust. Although God reveals Himself through natural and special revelation, His fullest revelation of Himself is found in Scripture, and so this is our best source. In it, God not only reveals Himself, He also tells us how we can know Him personally and grow in our relationship with Him. By applying the following steps, we can gain a true knowledge of God.

STUDYING BIBLICAL IMAGES OF GOD

The Bible describes God in many different ways from Genesis to Revelation. It presents His attributes (or characteristics) using descriptions of His nature and His activities primarily in the Old Testament, while the New Testament's main additions are the triune nature of God (see Pocket Principle™ #5, *The Trinity And God The Father*) and the embodiment of Him in Jesus Christ (see Pocket Principle™ #6, *Jesus, God the Son*).

> As Christians, our relationship with God should be the most important relationship in our lives.

God also reveals Himself in His names. There are several primary names for God used in the Bible. In the Old Testament He is called *El* (translated "God"), *Yehweh* (translated "LORD"), and *Adonai* (translated "Lord"). *El* seems to be used in contexts where God's power and justice are in view, such as in creation or the great flood. *Yehweh* is God's covenant name by which He revealed Himself to Israel (His people in the Old Testament). *Yehweh* is used primarily in contexts where God is acting graciously toward His people, such as in creating Eve for Adam or when He speaks to His people directly. Comparable names are used in the New Testament: *Theos* ("God") for *El* and *Kurios* ("Lord") for *Yehweh*. Often more insight is gained when the names of God are used in combination. For example, *El Shaddai* means "God Almighty," communicating the idea of God's power and strength. The attributes or descriptions of God in Scripture can be divided into two groups. The first group is composed of those attributes that we can share with God; attributes He calls us to emulate. For instance, God is holy, and we are called to holiness. "Be perfect [finished, complete, pure, holy], therefore, as your heavenly father is holy." (Matthew 5:48) Another of these attributes is love. God is love, and we are to love Him with all our heart, soul and mind and our neighbor as ourselves (Matthew 22:37-39). There are many more of these attributes, such as truthfulness, faithfulness, goodness, patience, mercy, justice, righteousness, etc.

> We need to be careful not to ignore any of God's attributes, and they must be kept in balance.

The other group of attributes is made up of those that we can never share with God. In these ways, God will always be different and greater than we are. For example, God is "Spirit." He does not have a body like we do. He is "self-existent." No one made Him and He is dependent on no one. We, and the rest of the universe, are created by God and are dependent on Him to continue to exist. Other attributes we can never share are His immutability, eternality, infinity, omniscience, omnipotence, omnipresence and sovereignty. (See word definitions in Exhibit entitled "Attributes of God.")

BALANCING GOD'S ATTRIBUTES

It is important to keep God's attributes in balance in our thinking; not to emphasize one attribute over another or to omit an attribute. For example, a person asks, "How can a loving God condemn people to hell?" Another person asks, "How can a holy God have anything to do with sinners?" Each of these questions isolates one attribute of God from the others. The truth is that God is both loving and holy, and He has demonstrated both His love and His holiness by sending His Son to die for us. If we focus on only one attribute, we will have a distorted view of God's character. The warning here is that we need to be careful not to ignore any of God's attributes, and they must be kept in balance.

In addition to keeping God's attributes in balance, it is helpful to have a general principle to use as we organize the attributes. The concept of God as our Father has been suggested as an organizing idea that properly blends His attributes. In Scripture God has revealed Himself as a father figure and believers as His children. Jesus taught His followers to address God as "Father" when praying (Matthew 6:9), and Paul says we have received the Spirit who prompts us to cry out to God, saying, "Abba, Father." (Romans 8:15)

God's attributes can also be organized around His three primary attributes: love, holiness and truth. For instance, God's grace, mercy and goodness can be thought of as parts of God's love. His justice, righteousness and wrath proceed from His holiness, and His faithfulness and veracity from His truth.

All of God's other attributes and all that He does must be consistent with each of these primary attributes. As an example, the salvation that God offers to mankind must be consistent with His love, holiness and truth. God's holiness is shown when He pours out His wrath against our sins on Christ, who is our substitute. His love is demonstrated by the fact that He pours out His wrath against our sins on Christ, instead of on us. His truth is revealed when He consistently does what He says He will do. In Isaiah 53:5-6 God said He would send a Messiah (Jesus) whom He would punish for our sins. All aspects of salvation are consistent with who God is.

LIVING CONSISTENTLY WITH THE TRUTH ABOUT GOD

There is more to gaining a true knowledge of God than can come from intellectual studies. It is also necessary to experience God, i.e. to interact with Him in the everyday affairs of life. In a similar way, can we truly know a person by just reading about him in a book? We might learn many good, bad and interesting things about him from the book, but can we really be sure we know him if we have never met or spent time with him? The answer is obvious. Personal experience is necessary to truly know a person. The same is true about knowing God. We have to have a real relationship with Him for that to happen.

And He invites us to experience Him. James 4:8 says that if we draw near to God, He will draw near to us. What an incredible offer! One way we can draw near to Him is through prayer. By setting aside time in each day to talk with and listen to God our relationship with Him grows as we learn how to be still before Him, how to pray requests that are consistent with His will and how to distinguish His thoughts from our own. In John 14:21 Jesus gives another invitation to experience God. This Scripture tells us that if we obey Jesus' commands, it shows that we love Him. Jesus goes on to say that He will show His love for us in return by revealing Himself to us. Another great offer: Out of your love for Me, obey Me and I will manifest Myself to you! Now He doesn't say *how* He will show Himself to us. It could be a direct revelation of Himself or an indirect meeting of our needs in some unexpected way. God is not limited in how He might reveal Himself, but He has promised that we will come to know Him better and better, and His promise is trustworthy.

James 4:8 says that if we draw near to God, He will draw near to us. What an incredible offer!

As we experience God, we also need to choose to live in a way that is consistent with what He has revealed about Himself. Jesus says in John 8:31-32, "If you hold to my teaching, you are really my disciples. Then you will know the truth, and the truth will set you free." The message of this passage is that to really know the truth and be set free by it, we must first hold to or obey the truth that God has already shown us. In other words, when we obey what we know of God's Word, He is faithful to affirm it as true and teach us even more truth and change our lives for the better (set us free) through it. Once again, He has given us a great promise.

An Old Testament example of God's people being challenged to live consistent with the truth God has revealed to them is found in Joshua 24:14-21. God had revealed that He was the only true God to Israel in many miraculous ways. Therefore, when Joshua challenged the Israelites to serve God wholeheartedly and throw away the idols they brought with them from Egypt, their response (at least initially) was to discard the idols and serve God only.

A more current example of living consistent with truth is the challenge for us to live the truth that God is sovereign. For example, when a Christian gives thanks (in all things) even in the midst of difficulty (I Thessalonians 5:18; Romans 8:28) she is affirming that she knows God and believes that He is sovereign and able to care for His own. The Christian's life is reflecting the truth about God!

CONCLUSION

Because of the critical importance of how we think and feel about God we need to make every effort to do the things that lead to a true knowledge of God. We should study biblical images of God, balance the attributes of God and live consistently with what God has revealed about Himself.

End Note:

(1) A.W. Tozer, *The Knowledge of the Holy* (New York: Harper & Row, 1961), 9.

The Attributes Of God

GOD'S ATTRIBUTES WE CAN SHARE

The characteristic of God whereby He is:

TRUTHFUL: God is completely honest, genuine. John 1:14, 14:6

FAITHFUL: God is completely trustworthy and loyal to His children.
II Thessalonians 3:3; Isaiah 49:7; I Peter 4:19

LOVING: God is unconditionally compassionate, caring and devoted toward us.
His ultimate love was demonstrated by Jesus on the cross. I John 3:16, 4:9-10

GOOD: God is complete, right, excellent. Luke 18:19; Exodus 33:19

PATIENT: God demonstrates forbearance and endurance towards mankind.
II Peter 3:9

MERCIFUL: God is actively good toward those in distress. He does not treat
them as they deserve because of their sin. Romans 9:15-16; Exodus 33:19

HOLY: God is totally pure, perfect and complete. He is set apart and above all
His creation. Exodus 15:11; Isaiah 6:1-4

JUST: God always acts in a right and fair manner. John 5:30; Psalms 89:14, 97:2

RIGHTEOUS: God is morally perfect. Psalms 89:14, 97:2

GOD'S ATTRIBUTES WE CAN NEVER SHARE

The characteristic of God whereby He is:

SPIRIT: God is invisible, immaterial, does not have a body. Genesis 1:2; John 4:24; I Timothy 1:17; Colossians 1:15

SELF-EXISTENT: God is everlasting; has no beginning and no end. Exodus 3:14; Psalm 90:2

IMMUTABLE: God is unchanging in His character and in His purposes. Numbers 23:19; James 1:17; Hebrews 13:8

ETERNAL: God is everlasting and immortal. Psalm 90:2; Isaiah 40:28; I Timothy 1:17

INFINITE: God is unlimited. He is above time and space, unlike His creation. I Kings 8:27; Psalm 147:5; Jeremiah 23:24

OMNISCIENT: God is all-knowing. He knows Himself and all things perfectly (and exhaustively). He knows all the possibilities and probabilities. Psalm 139:1-4, 147:5; Isaiah 40:13,14

OMNIPOTENT: God is all-powerful and almighty. Isaiah 40:21-26; Jeremiah 32:17; Job 42:2; Matthew 19:26

OMNIPRESENT: God is present everywhere at once. Psalm 139:7-12; Acts 17:24,27,28

SOVEREIGN: God has supreme authority, reign and control over His created order. Ephesians 1:11; Isaiah 46:9-11

Attributes Of God

IMPORTANT to Leader: Answers and notes to leaders are in gray, italicized text.

GOAL:

For a disciple to understand how God's attributes are relevant to her life.

GETTING STARTED:

On a human level, what do we need from our fathers? Brainstorm about what these needs are.

Transition: We have a loving Father in heaven, whom we can count on because of His character.

STUDYING TOGETHER:

Read Matthew 14:22-33.

1. What attributes of God (Jesus) did the disciples experience in this passage?

   His power, His sovereignty, love and care for them, His faithfulness, His worthiness to be worshipped, etc. Ask students to refer to Exhibit "Attributes of God" if necessary.

   Statement by Leader: We can often see many of God's attributes in one situation.

Read Luke 7:36-50.

2. The Pharisee is a respected religious leader, and the woman is probably a prostitute. How are God's love and His justice worked out in this situation?

   Toward the woman: Jesus' act of forgiving her demonstrated His love for her and at the same time, satisfied His justice (the sin required repentance). Toward the Pharisee, Jesus' act of exposing his self-righteousness was loving (although it is doubtful the Pharisee saw it that way!) and helped the Pharisee face the reality of his sin. Without this, there could not be repentance, which justice requires. The act also revealed Jesus' justice which demanded that sin be renounced.

   Statement by Leader: Sometimes we can find seemingly contradictory aspects of God's character in one situation.

Read James 4:8.

3. What does God require and promise in this verse?

    Requires: That we draw near to Him; seek Him, pray and read His Word; seek to build a relationship with Him. Promises: That He will draw near to us; be with us; meet us when we seek Him.

Read John 14:21.

4. What does God require and promise?

    Requires: That we show that we love Him by obeying His commandments. Promises: That He will show His love for us by revealing Himself to us; by letting us get to know Him, build an intimate relationship with Him.

Read John 8:31-32.

5. What does it mean to "hold to my teaching" (NIV) or "continue in my Word" (NAS)?

    It means to obey consistently, over the long-haul. Suggests the idea of endurance.

6. What does He promise if you obey His Word consistently?

    It would demonstrate that you are truly His disciple, and you will know the truth.

    NOTE: In the Greek, the verb "know" in verse 32 carries the connotation of "knowing from experience."

7. How does experiential knowledge set a disciple free?

    Sets him free from sin and its temptation; sets free to live a righteous life and to please God; sets free to live at rest according to Hebrews 12:11.

LOOKING AT REAL LIFE:

In Acts 4 Peter and John are brought before the Sanhedrin (Jewish ruling body).

Now **Read Acts 4:18-31.**

8. How do Peter and John show their obedience to God?

    Acts 4:20ff

9. Describe what happened as a result of their obedience to God.

    They were not afraid; and see list in verse 31.

10. What was God's response to what Peter and John did?

    He shook their meeting place. They were filled with the Holy Spirit, (1) and spoke the Word boldly.

11. What did this response reveal about God to Peter and John and other believers?

    He approved of the stand they took. He would empower them to continue ministering. He would be "with them" (on their side).

LOOKING AT MY LIFE:

Think of a situation in your life in which you have grown in your personal experience with God as a result of obeying Him. Please share with the group.

Leader: Close in prayer praising God for His attributes, specifically the ones mentioned by group members. Point out that the Exhibit entitled "Attributes of God" is a resource for students.

End Note for Leader:

(1) The filling of the Holy Spirit is discussed in The Holy Spirit *document in this series.*

Correcting False Views Of God

INTRODUCTION

God's character is described in detail throughout His Word. Sometimes when we read Scripture, we have a difficult time reconciling the words that describe God with our own understanding of God. This may happen because our knowledge of God has been influenced by factors which caused us to develop a false view of Him. For us to grow in relationship with God, we must correct our false views.

Luke, age 30, grew up in an average middle class family. They attended church and Sunday school together every week. Luke has memorized Scripture verses which he quotes regularly and can name, in order, every book of the Bible.

Each of us is specially created by God with our own personality, temperament, gifts and abilities. We each live in our own unique environment. Our inherent traits combined with our environmental influences will determine how we interpret our experiences. This is how we make sense of our world. However, we do have natural limits; not enough brain power to know everything or enough time to experience everything. Our desire to protect ourselves emotionally conspires with our own sinfulness to slant our perception of reality. Past experiences will have an effect on our present point of view. With different variables providing input, we do not always interpret our experiences correctly.

> It is common to project the strengths and weaknesses of our parents onto God.

Luke has a very likeable personality, is outgoing and charming, and relates to women better than men. He is also very gifted musically. He sings and plays several instruments well. He is the minister of music at his church.

Unfortunately, our human tendency to misinterpret our experiences can affect our view of God as well. It is common to project the strengths and weaknesses of our parents onto God. It is also common to project other human characteristics onto God. False views of God can make it very difficult to relate to Him. Because of these false views, many people are struggling to establish and maintain a healthy, Biblical view of God.

Luke's father was distant and detached when Luke was growing up. He was a quiet, solemn man who rarely smiled.

Some of the common false views of God are a God who is impossible to please; a God who is emotionally distant; a God who is condemning; a God who is unreliable and a God who abandons.

Although Luke appears to have an excellent Christian walk, he views God as emotionally distant and impossible to please. He constantly feels as though he is letting God down and that God is not particularly interested in him. He secretly believes that he has failed God. He has trouble referring to God as "Father."

The situation is not hopeless. Once we are aware that our views of God are false, we can take some concrete steps towards correcting them.

Luke recently joined a small men's Bible study with several men from outside his church. As the group progressed, the men began to bond emotionally and share with each other more deeply. Luke became aware that many of the men in the group had a different view of God than he did. They were convinced God loved them and they seemed to have an intimate relationship with Him. Luke was surprised by this and gradually began to share his views of God in the group.

It is as though we have a God we know with our thoughts and a different God we know with our emotions.

IDENTIFY FALSE VIEWS

The first step is to *identify* our false views of God. Exactly what false character traits are we assigning to Him? We must consider ideas that we wrestle with or ideas that we have trouble believing are true. It can be helpful to look at a list of false views that people typically have about God. Some of those are mentioned in the paragraph above, but this list is by no means exhaustive. It frequently happens that we have two competing views of God; the view presented in Scripture and the view based on how we have interpreted our experiences with God. It is as though we have a God we know with our thoughts and a different God we know with our emotions.

One of the older men in the group, Richard, helped Luke realize that his views of God did not line up with Scripture. He encouraged Luke to explore more fully his views of God.

The next step in correction is to *identify the sources* of our false views of God. How did these false views arise? It is helpful to realize that most of our false views are based on our early life experiences, mainly involving our families. After listing our false views of God, we must spend some time identifying and describing the *feelings* that these views cause. For some of us this will take some time, but for others the feelings will quickly surface. We must then ask ourselves some questions. "Have I ever felt these same feelings earlier in life? When and in what circumstances did I feel them?" These experiences and the feelings they cause will often taint our interpretation of our experiences with God.

As Luke talked more about his views of God with Richard and the group, he began to feel sadness over the lack of connection in his relationship with God. In a fairly short time, Luke was also able to connect those feelings of sadness to his relationship with his father. He realized that he had assumed God was just like his earthly father, cold and distant.

REINTERPRET OUR EXPERIENCES

The third step in correction is to *reinterpret our experiences*. We must look back at the experiences that contributed to the development of our false views of God and ask Him to show us what He was trying to accomplish in those times. We must also ask Him to reveal His heart towards us. We should try to use our head (scriptural) knowledge of God when asking Him for these revelations. Feelings can be unreliable and we need to be objective, so we may also need someone else to help us to see God's perspective. It is important to be honest with God about our emotions during this process. If we are angry with God we should express that anger to Him. He knows our hearts anyway, and if we are honest with Him, He can heal our hearts.

> We must create new experiences to help us internalize God's truth.

As Luke continued to process his feelings, he leaned on Richard a lot for feedback and guidance. He realized that he was angry at God for the lack of connection he had with his father. He felt God had deprived him. Richard helped Luke express his anger to God. He helped Luke explore his past openly and pointed out instances where it had appeared God was there and caring deeply for Luke in the midst of his need. They prayed together for insight, grieved at Luke's loss and talked for hours about God's characteristics.

DETERMINE AND REINFORCE A RIGHT VIEW OF GOD

The fourth step in correction is to *determine and reinforce a right view* of God. One important way to accomplish this is to meditate on the truth of who God is. We must read and study Scripture, think about it, ponder it and absorb it into our hearts and minds. We must ask others to help us recognize when we begin to rely on our feelings; feelings that are contrary to what God has revealed about Himself in Scripture. We must create new experiences to help us internalize God's truth. This means that in spite of what our feelings may be telling us, we will make faith-choices based on the truth of God's Word.

Richard became a substitute father for Luke during this time. Luke began to experience the way a connected father would interact with his son. Richard helped Luke learn for the first time how to read Scripture with his heart. He directed Luke to Bible passages that would tell him of God the Father's love for his children. Gradually, Luke began to let go of his false views of God and to develop a relationship with God that stunned him with its intimacy.

For some of us, correcting false views of God will be a relatively easy process. For others, the process may take longer and be a more difficult journey. Developing and reinforcing right views of God can make a tremendous difference in our relationship with Him. Right views of God will allow us to be more obedient to Him and more compassionate and loving to others. They will deepen and expand our adventure of living with God.

Luke is now able to say with absolute certainty, "God the Father loves me."

Correcting False Views Of God

Correcting false views involves several steps:

1) Identify false views of God that you have:

    a. We often have two competing views of God.
    b. One view is the one presented in Scripture. The other is the one based on how we interpret our experiences with God. (Note David's change of perspective when he took his struggles to God in Psalm 73.)

2) Identify the sources of these false views:

    a. Most false views are based on early life experiences, primarily involving our families.
    b. These experiences often taint our interpretation of our experiences with God.

3) Reinterpret your experiences:

    a. As you look at the experiences that contributed to the development of your false view of God, ask Him to show you what He was trying to accomplish in those times and what His heart is toward you (Romans 8:28).
    b. You may need help being objective since it is easy to just react to your feelings, which may be unreliable. Ask someone else to help you see God's greater purposes in your life.

4) Determine and reinforce right views of God:

    a. Meditate on the truth of who God is.
    b. With the help of others, recognize when you begin relying on your feelings instead of what God has revealed about Himself in Scripture.
    c. Create a new experience to help you internalize truth. This involves making a faith-choice based on the truth of God's Word, in spite of what your feelings say.

Correcting False Views Of God

IMPORTANT to Leader: Answers and notes to leaders are in gray, italicized text.

GOALS:

For a disciple to understand some of the common false views of God and ways to correct them.

For a disciple to begin to identify and correct any false views of God he may have.

GETTING STARTED:

Read John 11:1-6,17-21,32.

1. What negative message might Jesus' decision in verse 6 have sent to His disciples?

   That He was uncaring and too busy to care for everyone's needs.

2. What false views could Martha and Mary have held about Jesus regarding the death of their brother?

   That He was uncaring because He waited too long. That God's power was limited to His personal presence. That God's power was constrained by death.

Read John 11:33-44.

3. What did Jesus' actions in these verses indicate about the God that Mary and Martha were serving?

   God was caring, compassionate, loving, powerful, personal, and redemptive.

Transition: As we see in this Biblical example, it is not unusual for people to misinterpret experiences, and therefore, have a false view of God.

STUDYING TOGETHER & LOOKING AT REAL LIFE:

Our human tendency to misinterpret experiences affects our view of God.

Below is a chart with headings: Experiences, False View of God and Right View of God. The False View of God has been completed for you. Work as a group to complete the other 2 columns. (Working on a flip chart or on a dry erase board may be easiest.)

*Leader: Only **one** example of each type of experience is listed below under "Possible Experience." There are **numerous kinds** of experiences that can lead to any one false view of God.*

Possible Experience	False View of God	Right View of God
Overly critical judgmental parent	**Harsh, judgmental**	*Just, but loving (Psalm 103:8-13)*
Emotionally distant parent	**Emotionally distant**	*Intimate, accessible (Hebrews 4:15-16)*
Let down by friends at significant times in life	**Unreliable**	*Faithful (II Timothy 2:13)*
Significant peer rejection	**Abandons**	*Always present (Hebrews 13:5b)*
Critical, perfectionistic authority figure	**Impossible to please**	*Gives grace (Romans 5:1-2)*

LOOKING AT MY LIFE:

Read the Exhibit entitled *Correcting False Views Of God* (pg. 38). Answer the questions below, and share with the group if you feel comfortable doing so.

Which of the false views discussed do you identify with most? (Of course, these are just some of the most common false views. Share another if you see it in your life.)

As far as you can tell, what do you think is the source(s) of this view in your life?

As you look back at the experiences in your life that contributed to your false view of God, how might they have been interpreted differently?

The Trinity And God The Father

Most of us can't remember being a baby. But we all were, even if there is no hard evidence, (such as those embarrassing photos parents often bring out at holidays). As babies, we formed critical ideas about ourselves and the world around us. Sociologists and psychologists tell us that one of the most basic ideas that we developed was the understanding that we were distinct, separate from the world around us. We are different from everyone else, even our parents. Our hands were our hands, not somebody else's. There was an "us" and there was a "not us."

This concept of being distinct and separate is also true of God. He is different from His creation. He is different from us and all the universe. Nothing can quite compare to Him nor entirely explain Him. In order to develop a true relationship with God we need to understand this. We must realize that "God Is Who He Is." To understand who God is, we must understand what He has said about Himself.

> The persons of the Trinity relate to each other in a living and vital way.

God reveals aspects of His character and rule through the natural world. The amazing complexity, order, beauty and grandeur of the physical world tell us something of God's majesty. But He especially tells us about Himself through Scripture. One unique way that God has revealed Himself in the Bible involves His three-in-one nature. The Church calls this three-person aspect of God: "the Trinity." Admittedly this is a difficult concept to grasp, but it is central to understanding Him. We can know God more fully by studying how He has revealed Himself through each Person of the Trinity.

THE TRINITY

Deuteronomy 6:4 declares, "The Lord is our God, the Lord is one!" The Scriptures are very clear, there is only one God. Yet He exists in three eternal and equal persons who are the same in essence, but uniquely distinct from one another. The Scriptures place the three persons of the Trinity together as equals: the Father, the Son and the Holy Spirit (Matthew 28:19; I Peter 1:2; I Corinthians 12:4-6; II Corinthians 13:14).

The Trinity is a great mystery to us. We cannot fully understand how God can be one God and three persons, because we have no complete and exact comparison for this concept. Many things about our infinite God are hard to understand from our finite, human vantage point (cf. Isaiah 55:8-9). Yet we can define and believe this because the Bible teaches it. Just as we do not have to understand electricity in order to believe it exists and to use it, so the Trinity exists despite our inability to fully comprehend this truth.

Consider water. It is one substance (H_2O), but exists in three forms: liquid (water), gas (steam) and solid (ice). Perhaps it is helpful to note that in a similar way God is one being who is expressed in the three persons of the Trinity. Unlike H_2O, however, the persons of the Trinity relate to each other in a living and vital way. Generally speaking, within the Trinity, God exhibits three roles: God the Father initiates and plans, God the Son executes the plans, and God the Holy Spirit applies the plans to believers. Within the Trinity, unity is brought about by the Son submitting to the Father and the Holy Spirit submitting to the Son and the Father. God the Father has, in turn, given all authority to the Son to carry out the divine plans.

GOD THE FATHER

As the first person of the Trinity, God the Father shows His fatherly relationship toward both believers and non-believers through Creation and His common goodness to all the world. The Scriptures say that God the Father causes His sun to rise on the evil and the good, and sends rain on the just and the unjust. He provides for the animals and the fields, for the people of His Kingdom and even the people who oppose Him (Matthew 5:45, 6:25-33, 7:9-11; Luke 6:35; Hebrews 12).

Furthermore, God the Father demonstrates that He has a unique relationship with believers. God draws us to Himself, graciously bringing us into His family as children (John 6:44, 1:12; I John 3:1). Indeed, God has sent the Spirit of His Son into our hearts, so that we may truly call Him, "Abba! Father!" (Romans 8:15-16; Galatians 4:6-7) It is a great and humbling mystery to be called children of the Living God and to be made co-heirs with Jesus Christ the Son (Romans 8:17).

> This adoption by God the Father leads to special privileges and responsibilities for His children.

This adoption by God the Father leads to special privileges and responsibilities for His children. In Ephesians 1:3-14, we see that God the Father freely forgives us and provides every good thing we need. He has special intentions for us—to be holy and blameless—and has revealed His plan to us in Scripture. As a perfect Father, He has assured us of our place in His love by giving us the Holy Spirit as a guarantee of our inheritance as His children. With all the joy and security of beloved children, we have free access to God the Father through faith (Ephesians 3:12).

Likewise, God the Father has endowed His children with responsibilities such as obeying His Word (John 14:21) and representing Him as messengers of reconciliation to the world (II Corinthians 5:20). As members of His family, we are to be a part of His church and to respond to Him in praise and worship (Hebrews 10:24-25; I Peter 2:9).

As we study who God is, we come to understand more of His character and His nature. Through the Scripture, we learn that God is both transcendent (beyond our understanding) in the mystery of His Trinity, and He is immanent (totally accessible) as our heavenly Father. With whole hearts we can call on Him as Lord and Father!

SUMMARY

It is important to understand what God has revealed about Himself in Scripture.

• God is a Trinity, existing in three eternal and equal persons who are one God.

• Although the Trinity cannot be fully understood, the Bible teaches us to believe.

• God the Father, Son and Holy Spirit fulfill different roles.

• God the Father is the first person of the Trinity.

• As His children, we have special privileges and responsibilities.

The Trinity And God The Father

IMPORTANT to Leader: Answers and notes to leaders are in gray, italicized text.

GOALS:

For the disciple to begin to understand the concept of the Trinity with a special focus on God the Father.

For a disciple to show appreciation and gratefulness for the kindness of God.

GETTING STARTED:

There are things we believe in that we can't understand. For example, we believe in and rely on electricity, but most of us don't understand exactly how it works. What are some other examples of things that we believe in and rely on that we don't understand?

How a car works, a computer, e-mail, etc.

Transition: There are many aspects of God that we believe in and rely on, but don't fully understand. One of these aspects is the Trinity.

STUDYING TOGETHER:

Read together:

The *Trinity* is one God (Deuteronomy 6:4) who exists in three persons. There are three eternal and co-equal persons in the Trinity, the same in essence but uniquely distinct from one another. The three persons of the Trinity are God the Father, Jesus the Son and the Holy Spirit.

Read I Peter 1:1-2.

1. How do you see the oneness of the Trinity shown in these verses?

   They are all working together toward the same goal. All are bringing people to salvation.

2. What different roles do you see the members of the Trinity playing in the salvation process?

   Father: chose, gave new birth; Son: brought about salvation through death and resurrection; Holy Spirit: sanctifies the person by applying salvation to his life. Sanctifies means to "set apart," to "make holy."

*To be read by the leader: In **general** the members of the Trinity play these roles:*

Father: initiates and plans

Son: executes the plans

Holy Spirit: applies the plans to believer's lives

Read John 8:28 and John 16:13-15.

3. What more do you learn about the inter-relationships between the Father, the Son and the Holy Spirit from these verses?

   The Son submits to the Father, only does what the Father does. The Holy Spirit submits to the Son.

To be read by the leader: This chain of submission (or better described as chain of service) reflects the unity within the Trinity.

The remainder of this lesson will focus on God our Father.

Read Romans 8:15-16.

4. God wants us to call Him father—"abba," which is an informal, endearing address such as "daddy" or "papa."

   How does a loving father ("abba") relate to His children?

   He is their authority. He provides, protects, directs, watches over, teaches, etc.

5. This passage refers to us being children of God, not slaves who fear. What are some of the advantages of being a child of God?

   Are secure, not afraid, motivated by love, want to please, feel accepted and free, etc.

Read Psalm 139:13-18.

6. Some people believe that their birth was an "accident." What do these verses say about this?

   No one's birth is an accident. God formed us in our mother's womb, and determined our days before we were born.

7. What does it mean to you that you are "fearfully and wonderfully made"?

   God used his marvelous knowledge and wisdom in creating us. We are not afterthoughts.

8. What do verses 17-18 tell you about the way God feels about you? (in the NIV, the word "to" may also be translated "concerning")

   God can't get me off His mind! God thinks about me all night long as I sleep… more times than the number of grains of sand on all the seashores.

Read Ephesians 1:3-9.

9. What do verses 4-5 tell you about God's desire to be a kind Father to you?

   Before you were born, God desired to have a relationship with you. He chose you to be one of His own before you existed. Out of love, God planned to adopt you as one of His children. Showing you kindness brings God great pleasure.

10. Look over verses 4-9 and list the words or phrases that indicate how God the Father seeks a relationship with you. (We, as believers, also have responsibilities in our relationship with God. These are described other places in Scripture.)

    Jesus Christ—He sent his Son to die for our sins so we might have a relationship with Him.

    Chose—God chooses to seek a relationship with us.

    Predestined—God plans to have a relationship with us.

    Adoption—God makes us one of His own family.

    Grace—We can't earn favor with God. He gives grace freely.

    His blood—Jesus was willing to die so we might have a relationship with the Father.

    Lavished—Our Heavenly Father covers us with His grace.

    Made known to us—God revealed the gospel about Jesus Christ to us so we might have a relationship with Him.

LOOKING AT REAL LIFE:

11. What things in life keep people from seeing God as a loving Father?

12. How does a relationship with God as Father meet a believer's needs?

LOOKING AT MY LIFE:

Spend some time thinking about the ways your Heavenly Father has been kind toward you. Share your list with the rest of the group.

Leader: Tell the group that they will be participating in the prayer time today using simple, sentence prayers to express their gratitude for the things God has done for them (the things they have written on their lists). The sentences they will be using are:

"Thank you God for _____" and "Thank you God for being _____."

Jesus, God The Son

Who is Jesus? This is the crucial question every person on earth must answer. Was He a great religious teacher or a madman? Was He God or just a man? There is much debate and controversy regarding His identity and His authority. Most people would like to believe that He was only a man who offered polite moralisms, making Him a role model for any civil society. But a careful study of His life and teachings eliminates this option.

C.S. Lewis, the famous English writer and philosopher, once said about Jesus: "You can shut Him up for a fool, you can spit at Him and kill Him as a demon; or you can fall at His feet and call Him Lord and God. But let us not come up with any patronizing nonsense about His being a great human teacher. He has not left that (option) open to us. He did not intend to." [1]

In truth, Jesus is God. One effective test of false doctrines and cults is to determine what they say about the person of Jesus Christ. As a rule, cults (groups generally considered to be misleading and harmful) and false churches deny the Biblical truth that Jesus is God the Son. For Christians, what we believe about Jesus is foundational to our salvation. Our knowledge of Him defines our understanding of God's character, purpose and relationship with us.

> What we believe about Jesus is foundational to our salvation.

Jesus Himself acknowledged that, although people can be deluded or confused about His identity, His true followers know Him and He knows them (Matthew 7:21-23, 16:13-17). It is therefore essential to understand Jesus as He truly is. In Scripture, God has revealed Himself to us, and this is our primary source of understanding who Jesus is. The Biblical testimony about Jesus gives us a many-sided picture of Him. By looking at what Jesus says about Himself and what other Biblical writers report about Him, we can know God more fully.

HIS DEITY

Few people today question Jesus' humanity; many deny His deity. Yet from the early records of God's revelation, Jesus has been announced as God Himself. For example, the prophet Isaiah proclaimed Jesus' deity, foretelling His birth and reign as "Wonderful Counselor, Mighty God, Eternal Father, Prince of Peace." (Isaiah 9:6, NAS)

Jesus Himself claimed to be God by declaring, "I and the Father are one." (John 10:30) Modern scholars and skeptics may argue what Jesus meant by this statement, but His contemporary audience understood it perfectly. The text says His enemies wanted to kill Him, "for blasphemy, because you, a mere man, claim to be God." (John 10:33)

Later, when His closest disciples were anxious during a time of intense opposition and uncertainty, Jesus reassured them by saying, "Anyone who has seen me has seen the Father." (John 14:9-13) In this situation, Jesus came to reveal the Father (John 1:18) and clearly proclaimed His identity as God and unity with God the Father so His followers would understand and be comforted by this truth.

In addition to the Old Testament evidence of Jesus' deity and His own claims to be God the Son, the New Testament writers also attest to His divine nature. Testifying to the supremacy of Christ and echoing the creation account of Genesis, the Apostle Paul writes, "For by Him all things were created: things in heaven and on earth, visible and invisible, whether thrones or powers or rulers or authorities; all things were created by Him and for Him." (Colossians 1:16) Clearly, the authority to create rests in God alone, and this authority Paul attributed to Jesus.

> Jesus laid aside His divine attributes and majesty, not using them while He was on earth in human form.

The writer of the Book of Hebrews sets forth an astounding profession of Jesus' deity, "The Son is the radiance of God's glory and the exact representation of His being, sustaining all things by His powerful word. After He had provided purification for sins, He sat down at the right hand of the Majesty in heaven." (Hebrews 1:3) In this passage, as well as many others throughout the New Testament, Jesus' claim to deity is central to His mission and ministry. Whether people reject or accept this claim, they cannot truly deny it.

HIS HUMANITY

Unlike His claim to deity, the fact of Jesus' humanity is not often opposed due to well-attested historical evidence. Nevertheless, the Bible records that Jesus is not merely a man, but uniquely God-Man. John 1:1-14 introduces this amazing and mysterious truth, referring to Jesus as the very expression, or Word, of God: "In the beginning was the Word, and the Word was with God, and the Word was God….The Word became flesh and made His dwelling among us. We have seen His glory, the glory of the One and Only, who came from the Father, full of grace and truth." To put it another way, Jesus is 100 percent God and 100 percent human, one person with two natures: human and divine.

While He was on earth, He lived a human life just like we do, with its pain, sorrows, joys and burdens; with its temptations, concerns and pleasures. His human experience has great significance for us. He identifies with us like a brother, a family member with whom we share the closest experiences. The Bible points out that this family bond with Jesus is central to His ministry in our lives and His joy in us. "Both the one who makes men holy and those who are made holy are of the same family. So Jesus is not ashamed to call them brothers." (Hebrews 2:11)

Like a true friend (the closest friend, John writes), Jesus understands us and shares everything with us (John 15:13-15). Like a perfect leader, He can sympathize with our weaknesses because He also was tempted, yet did not sin (Hebrews 4:14-16). Like the greatest friend, He sacrificed Himself for us, becoming our substitute in a way that only the holy God-Man could (II Corinthians 5:21; I Peter 3:18).

Finally, Jesus is our model of human godliness, of victorious suffering, and of obedient service. "Your attitude," the Apostle Paul tells the Philippian church, "should be the same as that of Christ Jesus." (Philippians 2:5; see also I Peter 2:21)

HIS MESSIAHSHIP

As we have seen from Biblical accounts of Jesus' deity and humanity, Jesus came to the world for a reason. Throughout the Old Testament, God promised to send a Messiah, or King, who would deliver His people. Two different, and apparently opposite, pictures of what this Messiah would be emerged from the prophets and the Scriptures. Isaiah 53:1-6 describes a "man of sorrows," a servant who suffers for the sins of God's people. But Isaiah also speaks of a kingly deliverer who will defeat God's enemies and establish an unending rule of peace (Isaiah 9:6).

The seemingly contradictory natures of these Messianic descriptions proved to be very troublesome for Jews who were primarily expecting a king who would provide political and cultural deliverance. In the struggle to reconcile these prophesies and promises, many failed to recognize the Messiah when He did appear. He did not "fit" their expectations because He first came as a suffering servant. Jesus claimed to be that Messiah, the Christ (or Anointed One). As the holy God-Man who laid down His life and rose again to glory, He alone has perfectly fulfilled the Biblical promise of the Messiah. He came first as a suffering servant, dying for our sins and reconciling mankind to God. "For even the Son of Man did not come to be served, but to serve, and to give His life as a ransom for many." (Mark 10:45; see also John 3:14-15; I Peter 3:18; I John 2:2)

> Through the Scriptures, God reveals that Jesus is fully God and fully human, the Messiah who came and is coming again.

Jesus also promised to come again as a conquering King who will deliver His people from the sin and ruin of this world. The Apostle Paul proclaimed the coming of God's Kingdom in these terms: "Then the end will come, when He hands over the Kingdom to God the Father after He has destroyed all dominion, authority and power. For He must reign until He has put all His enemies under His feet." (I Corinthians 15:24-25; see also John 14:1-3; Revelation 9:11-16, esp. v.16)

Who is Jesus? Through the Scriptures, God reveals that Jesus is fully God and fully human, the Messiah who came and is coming again. In Him, everything that is fully God is expressed in human form (Colossians 2:10). Therefore, we should worship Christ as God, look to Him as our model and trust in Him as our Savior.

SUMMARY

We can know God more fully by studying how He has revealed Himself as God the Son.

- The Old and New Testaments proclaim the deity of Jesus.

- Jesus Himself claimed to be God.

- Jesus is fully God and fully man.

- Because of His humanity, Jesus is able to identify with us, understand us, substitute for us, and be an example for us.

- Jesus claimed to be the promised Messiah who is both a suffering servant and a delivering king.

End Note:

(1) C.S. Lewis, *Mere Christianity* (San Francisco: Harper, 2001), 52.

Proofs For The Deity Of Jesus Christ

I. He is called God.

John 1:1,14,18, 10:30, 20:28   II Thessalonians 1:12
Romans 9:5   Titus 2:13
Colossians 2:9   Hebrews 1:3

II. He called God His Father, "making Himself equal with God." John 5:18

III. He was proclaimed to be the Son of God from heaven.

At His baptism: Matthew 3:16-17; Mark 1:10-11; Luke 3:21-22; John 1:32-34
At His transfiguration: Matthew 17:5; Mark 9:7; Luke 9:35; II Peter 1:17

IV. Jesus is the same as Yahweh in the Old Testament.

Compare Luke 1:76 with Malachi 3:1
Compare Romans 10:13 with Joel 2:32
Compare Romans 14:9-11 with Isaiah 45:23-25

V. Jesus has the attributes of Deity. These attributes are those which are only
true of God.

Eternal: Isaiah 9:6; John 1:1-2, 8:58, 17:5; Hebrews 1:8; Revelation 1:8
Omnipresent: Matthew 18:20, 28:20; John 3:13; Ephesians 1:23
Omniscient: Matthew 9:4; John 2:24-25, 6:64, 16:30, 21:17; Colossians 2:3
Omnipotent: Isaiah 9:6; Matthew 28:18; Philippians 3:21; Revelation 1:8
Immutable: Hebrews 1:10-12, 13:8

VI. Jesus performs the activities of Deity.

Creates: John 1:3-10; Colossians 1:16-17; Hebrews 1:2,3,10
Providence: Luke 10:22; John 3:35, 17:2; Ephesians 1:22; Colossians 1:17
Forgives sins: Matthew 9:27; Mark 2:5-10; Colossians 3:13
Raises the dead and judges them: Matthew 25:31-32; John 5:19-30; Acts 10:42,
    17:31; Philippians 3:21; II Timothy 4:1
Is the object of prayer and worship: Luke 24:51-52; John 5:23, 14:14; Acts 7:59,
    16:31; Philippians 2:10,11; Hebrews 1:6

Jesus, God The Son

GOAL:

For a disciple to have a clearer understanding of what the Scripture teaches about Jesus and to make a decision to make Christ more central in her life.

GETTING STARTED:

People over the centuries have had a variety of ideas about who Christ is. What are some of them?

Merely a good man, only God, only a prophet, a false prophet, a lunatic, a liar, etc.

Why do you think there is so much confusion about who Jesus is?

Transition: According to Christianity, Christ is the most important person who has ever lived in this world. Therefore, it is critical to know what the Bible teaches about Him.

STUDYING TOGETHER:

Different people attested to Jesus being God.

Read the following verses: John 1:1-3, John 10:30-33 and Colossians 1:16.

1. In each of these verses, what claim is made about Jesus? And who is making the claim?

    John 1:1-3—the Word, creator, God—the Apostle John

    John 10:30-33—One with God (the Father)—Jesus Himself

    Colossians 1:15—Image of the invisible God—the Apostle Paul

Read Philippians 2:5-8.

2. What does this passage tell us about Jesus?

    He is God (has a divine nature); laid aside His divine nature when He came to earth (vs. 7); became a man; became a servant; humbled Himself and was obedient even to death.

Leader: It is very important that the following points are clearly understood by the students.

Summary of points:
- **Jesus is both God and man.**
- **Jesus lived here on earth as a man and didn't use His divine nature during that time.**

Read Isaiah 53:1-5 and Isaiah 9:7.

3. What two contrasting pictures of the Messiah are found in these verses?

   Isaiah 53:1-6 sees Jesus as a suffering Servant for man's sin. Isaiah 9:7 presents Jesus as a kingly Deliverer from God's enemies.

   This apparent conflict is resolved in the New Testament.

Read Mark 10:45 and I John 2:2.

4. What picture of Jesus is given in each of these verses?

   A servant willing to give his life as a ransom; an atoning sacrifice for our sins

These verses picture what Jesus *did* at His first coming.

Read Revelation 19:11-16, esp. 16.

5. What picture of Jesus is given in these verses?

   A kingly Deliverer, a valiant Warrior

These verses picture what Jesus *will do* at His second coming. Both images, the one found in the Old Testament and the one found in the New Testament, are true: Jesus the Messiah is the suffering Servant and the kingly Deliverer!

LOOKING AT REAL LIFE:

6. Since Jesus is 100% God and 100% human and He laid aside His Divine nature to come to earth and live as a man to die as a sacrifice for our sins, what should the Christian's response to Him be?

   Worship, gratitude, amazement, willingness to follow, trust, obedience, etc.

7. Since Jesus will come back to get us and to bring justice to the world, what should the Christian's response be?

Anticipation, hope, endurance, amazement, worship, gives purpose to live, urgency to sharing the Gospel, etc.

LOOKING AT MY LIFE:

Gratitude and obedience are themes of a Christian's response to who Jesus is, what He has done and what He will do. Write a prayer to God expressing your gratitude and willingness to obey as you meditate on Jesus, your personal relationship with Him and what He has done for you.

Leader: Close in prayer yourself. Or, if you feel it is appropriate, ask 1 or 2 group members to read their prayers aloud if they feel comfortable doing so.

Also, point out to the students the Exhibit called "Proofs for the Deity of Jesus Christ," which they can study on their own.

Our Relationship With Christ Our Brother

Are we alone in the universe? For centuries people have wondered about the place of mankind in the vastness of space. Ancient astronomers calculated the movement of the constellations, wondering if there was some connection between the stars and people on earth. Now, with the development of long-range telescopes, the observable universe has expanded significantly. Some now believe there is a high probability that intelligent life exists elsewhere in the universe. (Supermarket tabloids certainly agree: reportings of UFO sightings and alien abductions are on the rise.) But this curiosity is more than a fringe movement, the scientific community routinely explores the possibility of life beyond our planet.

But not everyone is certain we'll make contact with other cosmic civilizations. Ever the cynic, the young protagonist of the comic strip "Calvin and Hobbes" quips that the only compelling evidence that there might actually be intelligent life elsewhere in the universe, is that "no one has ever tried to contact US!" But despite the various points-of-view, the question remains.

> God has placed mankind (not the rest of the cosmos!) at the apex of His creation, and "crowned him with glory and honor." (Psalm 8:3-5)

In 2003, Australian astronomers tried to calculate how many stars exist in the universe. (Every star could be the center of a system of potentially life-supporting planets.) Using two of the world's most powerful telescopes, these scientists observed 10,000 visible galaxies. By extrapolating this data to the limits of the known universe, they estimated the existence of an astonishing 70 sextillion stars! (For the mathematically challenged among us, that's a "7" followed by twenty-two zeroes!) [1] To begin to understand the immensity of this number, try to visualize all the grains of sand along every single beach, and in every single desert on the planet Earth. [2] Then multiply that amount by ten! This certainly suggests the possibility that, by comparison, we solar-system earth-dwellers are pretty insignificant.

But the Scriptures maintain another perspective. Instead of the myriad of stars pointing to humanity's insignificance in the universe, the Bible says that the vast number of stars actually affirms mankind's great worth and value. The psalmist considers the question: "When I consider Your heavens, the work of Your fingers, the moon and the stars which You have set in place, (I ask), 'What is man that you are mindful of him?'" The passage goes on to explain that God has placed mankind (not the rest of the cosmos!) at the apex of His creation, and "crowned him with glory and honor." (Psalm 8:3-5)

These verses (and others) remind us that God gave humans great worth amid all He created. In addition to placing mankind at the pinnacle of His created order, He did two other important things to underscore our value to Him: He created humans in His own image; and He honored mankind by sending Jesus, God's own Son, to earth as a man. We are not alone in the universe! God has chosen to live among us as one of us, not exactly like us, but significantly like us as a friend and brother! This 'living among us' has three encouraging implications.

GOD INITIATES TOWARD US.

God came to earth as Jesus to reconnect with us, initiating the restoration of a relationship that had been broken by sin (John 1:14). He searched for those who were willing to receive His love. (And though He returned to heaven, He continues to search through His Holy Spirit!) The Bible describes this search as like a man who has lost something of great value and who leaves everything to find what was lost (Parable of the Lost Sheep: Luke 15:1-7). The parable affirms that once the man finds what he lost, he experiences great joy (vv. 3-7)!

We are not alone. Though we have been separated from our Creator, He has not forgotten us! On the contrary, He is actively, diligently, looking for and seeking to rescue us, His lost sheep. We are the people He created in His image, for His glory. And once the relationship with any of us is restored, God rejoices and the angels join Him!

> Jesus put people at ease. Even the worst sinners felt that they could come to Him and He would befriend them.

This longing for a restored relationship has always been God's agenda, even when the relational distance seemed impossible to span. When God dwelt among His people in the Old Testament (Exodus 40:34-38) many of His words and actions made Him seem unapproachable (e.g. Exodus 19:1-25, 20:15-21). He often appeared to people in His awesome power, reminding Israel of His holy nature with repeated warnings that sinful men were forbidden to come near to Him. To further underscore this separation, there was an immense veil installed in the Hebrew Temple as a reminder that God could not be approached without an acceptable sacrifice.

But here's the Good News: Jesus WAS God's acceptable sacrifice! After His death on the Cross, the veil-barrier was removed! Anticipating this reconciliation, Jesus initiated toward people while He was on earth, embodying the love and grace of God the Father (John 1:16-18). Jesus put people at ease. Even the worst sinners felt that they could come to Him and He would befriend them. God's nature didn't change, He was still holy; but the relationship was restored at His initiative. Jesus was the embodiment of God the Father, showing God's love, grace, and approachability.

GOD IDENTIFIES WITH US.

Not only does God initiate toward us, He identifies with us completely. Scripture tells us that Jesus Christ was like us in his humanity (Philippians 2:7; Romans 8:3). It's incredible, but true: God was fully human in the person of Jesus, The Son! He functioned just like we do: He got hungry and ate, got tired and slept, worked, moved around, thought and had ideas, made decisions, experienced frustration, was limited by time and space, etc. But one way in which He was NOT like us, is that He never sinned. He was tempted, but He never sinned (Hebrews 4:15). (This sinlessness allowed Him to be the acceptable sacrifice we mentioned earlier and which we'll talk more about later.)

Because He was so much like us, we can know and have confidence that He understands us. He is totally empathetic. Jesus experienced the ups and downs of life just as we do. He experienced the joys and challenges of childhood, the teen years, and adulthood. He experienced good times and disappointments. He was wronged, suffering unjust persecution at the hands of people with selfish agendas. He was even betrayed by a friend. Because Jesus is able to empathize with us and our weaknesses, (without sinning), Scripture encourages us to approach His throne of grace in our times of need with hope, courage, boldness, and confidence (Hebrews 2:17-18, 4:15-16). He's like a best friend.

> But one way in which He was NOT like us, is that He never sinned. He was tempted, but He never sinned.

We all know what friendship is like, because we've all had a friend. I'll never forget my best friend from high school. We did everything together. We played sports (and rooted for the same teams), we went on double-dates, we took the same classes, we liked the same music, we ate the same fast-food; we could even finish each other's sentences. There were few secrets we didn't share, and he never betrayed a confidence. Don was more than a friend, he was like my own brother, (but without sibling rivalry).

It's hard to imagine Jesus being someone like that; but He is! In fact, He's better than any friend or brother we've ever had, or could ever imagine having. Because He was like us during His time on earth, we can call on Jesus as our brother and friend (Hebrews 2:11-12; John 15:13-15), and He will be there for us.

Because He was like us, we can also look to Him as a model for living the Christian life. But He's not some insufferable bore who's always correcting us or pointing out our mistakes. He's like the buddy who's always 'got our back,' the friend who can teach us how to throw a curve-ball, but who'll also fight for us and keep us out of trouble (if we'll let him) because He loves us. We can look to Jesus as this kind of friend, as we seek to emulate His righteous life because it's the best life, observing how He dealt with rejection and suffering, seeing how He related to God the Father, etc. And, as we follow His example, we find encouragement and camaraderie.

GOD SUBSTITUTES FOR US.

But He's more than a good companion. He's a friend who'll die for us. Here's the Bad News: because all people have sinned, all of us are awaiting God's judgment and wrath (Romans 3:23, 2:5). There is nothing anyone of us can do to work our way back into God's good graces. All of mankind's religious systems (attempts to placate God) ultimately fail. We spoke earlier of God's holiness and justice. We can't approach Him on the basis of our very best merits and deeds, because He is holy, totally unlike us. Apart from God's initiative and intervention, mankind has no hope, only the frightful prospect of God's judgment.

> Jesus is more than a good companion. He's a friend who'll die for us.

But don't forget the Good News! God intervened by sending His Son as a sacrifice and payment. (John the Baptist referred to Jesus as God's sacrificial lamb.) Because Jesus willingly became a man and lived a sinless life, He was an acceptable substitute for us (I Peter 3:18). When Jesus died a humiliating death on the cross, God poured out His wrath against our sins on His Son, rather than on us (Isaiah 53:6; I John 2:2).

The magnitude of this sacrifice shows the value God places on mankind (Mark 10:45). (The value of something is seen in the price a wise buyer is willing to pay for it.) God, who appointed us as the apex of His creation and made us in His Image, also died for us. God has done everything He could do to acknowledge the high worth of mankind and to make it possible for them to come back into a relationship with Him. Since this was not deserved in any way, all mankind ought to be humbled and in awe of what He has done in the Atonement.

Though humbled by the majesty and mercy of God, we are not alone in His vast universe, but comforted by His Presence! He has a cosmic plan and purpose for each of us that spans time and even creation itself. But at the heart of His plan is a relationship with Jesus, our friend and brother. It's impossible for us to fully comprehend all of this, but we aren't asked to completely comprehend it; God simply asks us to believe it and trust Him. But it's a belief that invites action: the decision to follow Jesus!

End Notes:

(1)Josh Gough,www.helium.com/items/128325-ascertain-answer-question-absolute

(2)Josh Gough, ibid.

Our Relationship With Christ Our Brother

IMPORTANT to Leader: Answers and notes to leaders are in gray, italicized text.

GOAL:

For a disciple to experience a sense of his own significance by understanding the humanity of Jesus.

GETTING STARTED:

What emotions would you feel if you were selected to be acknowledged by the President of the United States for an accomplishment that you achieved?

Pride, excitement, nervousness (fear), would feel honored, etc.

Why do you think you would feel these emotions?

Because of the status of the President; his important position, prestige, etc.

Transition: Someone far greater than the President has acknowledged you in significant ways: Jesus.

STUDYING TOGETHER:

Read Exodus 40:34-38.

1. Based on this passage, how did God manifest Himself to the Israelites?

   He was with them and led them. When the cloud of the Lord lifted above the tabernacle they traveled, but if the cloud didn't lift, they didn't travel. His fire led then by night.

Read Exodus 20:18-21.

2. Based on this passage, how do you think the Israelites perceived God?

   Frightening, very powerful, unapproachable

3. How do you think that affected how they related to God?

   They avoided Him, were afraid, wanted an intermediary, didn't approach Him.

Read Matthew 9:9-13.

4. In contrast, how did Jesus relate to people? (Remember, Jesus is God the Son.)

    With compassion, gentleness, sensitivity

5. How should people see God differently as a result of how Jesus related to people?

    See Him as approachable, as gracious, compassionate

*Leader: It is **important** that you read or clearly explain the point in the conclusion written below.*

Conclusion: Although God did change the way He related to His people from the Old Testament to the New, His character did NOT change. He was always loving and compassionate as well as holy and just.

Read Hebrews 2:14-18.

6. What do you think the phrase "shared in their humanity" means regarding Jesus?

    He came from heaven to earth and took on "flesh and blood." Jesus had a human body and lived a human experience, yet without sin.

7. In verse 17, we see that Jesus was "made like his brothers in every way." How does it make you feel that Jesus sees us as His brother (or sister)?

    It should instill trust and confidence in Him because we are from the same family. He is a brother who will stand up for us when we are persecuted. He is a brother who will stand by us when we need support and encouragement.

8. According to verse 18, why is Jesus qualified to help us during times of temptation?

    Because He knows what we are experiencing and what it takes to successfully fight temptation and walk in obedience. It wasn't easy for Him. In fact, this scripture shows us that He suffered greatly in the face of temptation (i.e., 40 days of fasting while being tempted by the devil; sweating drops of blood as He contemplated proceeding with the Father's plan for Him to go to the cross).

Read Hebrews 4:14-16.

9. Because Jesus experienced human temptations, overcame them without sin, and empathizes with us, we are encouraged to approach His "throne of grace with confidence." When you encounter great temptation and struggles, how do you usually approach Jesus?

   Some cower, some run, some wait...

10. According to verse 16, what will you receive when you approach Him in a "time of need"?

    We receive mercy and grace to help us overcome the temptations we encounter and the struggles we face.

Read I Peter 3:18.

11. According to this verse, what did Jesus do for you and what was its significance?

    He died for my sins, and made it possible for me to have a relationship with God. He made it possible for my sins to be forgiven.

LOOKING AT REAL LIFE:

12. Jesus initiated with us and is approachable, identified with us and was a substitute for us. How does this give us significance and worth?

    It tells me that I am worth pursuing; tells me that I'm so important that He would leave heaven for me; shows me that I'm so valuable that He sacrificed His life for me.

LOOKING AT MY LIFE:

Remembering that Jesus initiated with us and is approachable, identified with us and was a substitute for us, which of these ways that Jesus relates to us is most meaningful to you right now? Why?

*Leader: Ask group to pray a sentence prayer for each other about their needs.
A suggestion: Pray for the person on your right*

The Holy Spirit

"May the force be with you!" This now-familiar "benediction" of the Star Wars series has emerged as one of our cultural icons, characterizing an accompanying (albeit impersonal) power that is able to provide strength and comfort for life's challenges. Unfortunately, this is also how many Christians view the Holy Spirit. For them, the Holy Spirit is a mysterious "force" who somehow influences and impacts their lives. Admittedly, explaining the Person and work of the Holy Spirit can be daunting. But the rewards of understanding God through the Person of His Spirit far outweigh the difficulties.

Who is the Holy Spirit? Is this only another name for God? A force? An impersonal "it"? A separate personality? The Holy Spirit, like the idea of the Trinity, can be a difficult concept to understand. (In fact, almost all the cults stumble over the doctrine of the Holy Spirit, denying the existence of the Holy Spirit as God.)

Fortunately, we have the light of Scripture to show us God's will and reveal His truth. This is particularly valuable in our understanding of the Holy Spirit. At this point in history, God is invisible to our human perception. But though invisible, He is still there, and He is active in the affairs of our lives. Even though the wind is invisible we can describe it and see its effects. In a similar way we cannot see the Holy Spirit, but we can see Him in the Bible and witness His effects in the lives of believers (John 3:5-8). By studying how the Scriptures describe the Holy Spirit, we can know God more fully.

THE DEITY AND PERSONALITY OF THE HOLY SPIRIT

It is important to recognize that Scripture does not always give lengthy explanations or formal lessons about God and His Kingdom. The Bible is not an entire account or testimony of the acts of God toward His creation and His people. As such, we find that Scripture clearly teaches us about the Holy Spirit but does not set out to prove the deity and personality of the Holy Spirit. Instead, the Bible writers assume and teach the deity and personality of the Holy Spirit incidentally.

THE ROLE OF THE HOLY SPIRIT IN THE TRINITY

In many cultures, it is common when first meeting others to inquire about their family relations. By knowing someone's family name, it is possible to gain insights into the community roles and context of the new acquaintance. In a similar way, knowing how the Holy Spirit relates to the other persons of the Trinity gives us a better understanding of who He is.

As we read through the Bible, we can observe that God the Father's role is primarily that of planning and initiating. Jesus, God the Son, executes God the Father's plans. His Messianic role as suffering servant and delivering king is central to who He is. Finally, the Holy Spirit's role is to apply the plan to believers.

We can see these roles of the Trinity in the work of salvation. The Father plans and sends the Son. Jesus the Son executes the plan by dying on the cross for our sins and being raised from the dead. The Holy Spirit draws people to Christ and applies the benefits of salvation to them through His dwelling in their lives.

THE MINISTRIES OF THE HOLY SPIRIT

Sometimes the best way to relate to people is to learn what they do. Actions, as the saying goes, speak louder than words. The Holy Spirit takes many actions on behalf of believers, and it can help us understand God the Holy Spirit by considering these ministries.

The Holy Spirit automatically gives certain benefits to us when we first repent and believe in God's salvation. Titus 3:5 tells us, "He saved us through the washing of rebirth and renewal by the Holy Spirit." John 3:3-8 and Ephesians 2:4-5 also speak of this regenerative ministry. The Holy Spirit testifies to us about Christ's sacrifice and sets us apart for God's purposes when we are first saved (Hebrews 10:13-14). He indwells us, seals us, intercedes on our behalf and gives us spiritual gifts (Romans 8:9; Ephesians 1:13-14; Romans 8:26-27; I Corinthians 12:7-11). The Holy Spirit accomplishes each of these acts on our behalf at the moment of our salvation.

By studying how the Scriptures describe the Holy Spirit, we can know God more fully.

Other ministries of the Holy Spirit, however, are applied to believers only as we cooperate with Him. John tells us that the Holy Spirit can convict us of sin and teach us truth as we yield to His influence and power (John 16:8-11, 13-26). He guides us, empowers us and fills us, manifesting His grace in our lives as we seek God's will (Galatians 5:16-18; Acts 1:8; Ephesians 5:18). In essence, the Holy Spirit walks with us, affecting us throughout our lives by an ongoing process of making us holy (Hebrews 10:13-14).

The Holy Spirit not only works in the lives of believers, but He also convicts "the world of guilt in regard to sin and righteousness and judgment," making people ready to hear our Gospel message (John 16:8-11). Finally, the Holy Spirit inspired the Scriptures, literally "breathing" God into the writers. He is the ultimate source and authority of the Bible (II Timothy 3:16; II Peter 1:20-21).

> A close relationship with God and a humble, teachable attitude are hallmarks in the life of a person who knows how to be filled with the Spirit.

There is an important distinction that needs to be understood between the indwelling of the Holy Spirit and the filling of the Holy Spirit in the life of the believer.

The indwelling of the Holy Spirit occurs at the time of salvation: the Spirit enters the new believer's life (Acts 2:38; Romans 8:9; I Corinthians 12:13; Ephesians 1:13-14). This is an automatic, "once for all," permanent experience. The Spirit is in the believer's life to accomplish the functions mentioned above: sets aside for holy purposes (Hebrews 10:13-14), seals (Ephesians 1:13-14), intercedes (Romans 8:26-27), gives gifts (I Corinthians 12:7-11), etc.

The filling of the Holy Spirit describes what happens after salvation when a believer submits himself fully to everything he understands to be God's will. With this submission, the Holy Spirit fills the believer by guiding and empowering him to do the will of God. Because all believers struggle to stay fully submitted to God, the filling of the Holy Spirit must be repeated again and again (e.g. Acts 4:23-41, especially vs. 31).

In Ephesians 5:18b, which says "...be filled with the Spirit," the Greek verb "to be filled" is in the present progressive tense and means "to be filled over and over." Therefore, this command is telling believers that they are to be filled with the Spirit again and again. Understanding how to be filled with the Spirit (or how to walk in the Spirit) is critical to growing as a Christian. A close relationship with God and a humble, teachable attitude are hallmarks in the life of a person who knows how to be filled with the Spirit consistently.

Therefore, we should be humble and grateful because of who the Holy Spirit is and what He does in our lives. He is a personal God who is at work in our lives, helping us as we strive to obey and follow Him. We must seek Him in Scripture and in prayer, continuing a lifelong process of cooperating with Him.

SUMMARY

We can know God more fully by studying how He has revealed Himself as God the Holy Spirit.

- Scripture assumes and teaches the deity and personality of the Holy Spirit incidentally.

- The role of the Holy Spirit is better understood in relation to the roles of the other persons of the Trinity.

- The Holy Spirit draws people to Christ and applies the benefits of salvation to them through His indwelling.

- Some of the ministries of the Holy Spirit are automatically applied to the believer at salvation.

- Other ministries of the Holy Spirit are applied only with the believer's cooperation.

- We should humbly and gratefully cooperate with the Holy Spirit throughout our lives.

The Deity Of The Holy Spirit

I. **He is called God.** Acts 5:3,4; I Corinthians 3:16

II. **Attributes of God are ascribed to Him.**

Life-giving: Romans 8:2
Truth: John 16:13; I John 5:6
Love: Romans 15:30
Holy: Ephesians 4:30
Eternal: Hebrews 9:14
Omnipresent: Psalm 139:7-10
Omniscient: John 14:26, 16:12,13
Omnipotent: Luke 1:35; Job 33:4; Zechariah 4:6

III. **Works of God are ascribed to Him.**

Creating: Genesis 1:2
Regenerating: Titus 3:5
Inspiring Scripture: II Peter 1:21
Raising the dead: Romans 1:4
Begetting Christ: Luke 1:35
Sanctifying: II Thessalonians 2:13

IV. **Words and works of the Holy Spirit are considered words and works of God.**

Compare Isaiah 6:8-10 with Acts 28:25-27
Compare Exodus 16:7 and Psalm 95:8-11 with Hebrews 3:7-9
Compare Genesis 1:27 with Job 33:4
Compare Jeremiah 31:31-34 with Hebrews 10:15-17

V. **The Holy Spirit is associated with other persons of the Trinity as an equal.**

In instructions about baptism: Matthew 28:19
In a benediction: II Corinthians 13:14
In a salutation: I Peter 1:2

The Personality Of The Holy Spirit

I. **Attributes of personality are ascribed to the Holy Spirit.**

   A. Intellect
      I Corinthians 2:10,11: knows and searches the things of God
      Romans 8:27: possesses a mind
      I Corinthians 2:13: teaches

   B. Emotions
      Ephesians 4:30: can be grieved
      Romans 15:30: can love

   C. Will
      I Corinthians 12:11: distributes gifts
      Acts 16:6-11: directs Paul in his ministry
      Acts 15:28: "It seemed good to the Holy Spirit."

II. **Use of personal pronouns when describing the Holy Spirit.**

   A. John 16:14, 15:26, 16:7-8; I Corinthians 12:8-11; Romans 8:16,26; Ephesians 1:14

   B. Though the Greek work for "spirit" is neuter, a masculine pronoun is used to describe the Holy Spirit in each of these passages.

III. **He performs acts proper to personality. (Refer to Scriptures listed above for references which include these acts of the Holy Spirit.)**

He searches, knows, speaks, testifies, reveals, convinces, teaches, commands, strives, moves, helps, guides, creates, recreates, sanctifies, inspires, makes intercession, orders the affairs of the church, performs miracles, raises the dead, reproves, guides into truth, restrains, directs mankind in His service, calls humans into service, glorifies Christ, works…

IV. **He is affected as a person by the acts of others.**

   A. He is resisted, tempted, insulted, grieved, blasphemed, lied to, obeyed and reverenced. (Refer to Scriptures listed above for references which include these acts of the Holy Spirit.)

   B. If He was only an influence He would not be susceptible to such treatment.

The Holy Spirit

GOAL:

For a disciple to understand the role of the Holy Spirit and cooperate with what He is doing.

GETTING STARTED:

Imagine that you are on a long hike, and you are lost. When you first realize you are lost, how do you feel?

Frustrated, irritated, afraid, nervous, etc.

What will you do on your next hike to keep from getting lost?

Take a map, directions, a cell phone, a compass. Best of all, take a guide, someone who knows the trail.

Transition: God has graciously provided a perfect Guide for us in the Christian life: the third person of the Trinity, the Holy Spirit. We will be studying Him in this lesson.

STUDYING TOGETHER:

1. What three individuals are found in John 15:26?

   God the Father ("Father"), Jesus Christ ("I", "me"), and the Holy Spirit ("Counselor", "Spirit of truth").

2. Describe the relationship between the Father, Son, and Holy Spirit with the help of Galatians 4:6 and Luke 3:22.

   One God, but three persons in the Godhead who are co-equal and co-eternal. In general, what are their roles? Members of the Trinity have different roles: The Father plans and initiates. The Son executes the plans. The Holy Spirit applies the plans to believers.

3. Using the following scriptures, describe the ministries of the Holy Spirit in the life of the believer:

   - Acts 2:38—What is given by God at the time of salvation?
     Gift of the Holy Spirit: When a person "receives the gift of the Holy Spirit" it means that the Holy Spirit comes to live/dwell inside of the person.

- John 16:13-15, 14:26—What does the Holy Spirit teach believers?
  He teaches and guides believers in the truth.

- John 16:8-11—According to these verses, what does the Holy Spirit do?
  He brings conviction concerning sin, righteousness and judgment.

- Galatians 5:16-18—How does the Holy Spirit impact believers' daily lives?
  He guides us in daily living, away from sinful desires, empowers to overcome sin.

- Acts 1:8—What is the Holy Spirit's role in helping believers witness?
  He gives us power to share the good news.

- Hebrews 10:13-15—What is the Holy Spirit in the process of doing in the lives of believers?
  He is sanctifying us—that is, He is helping us become more like Christ in character and conduct.

- Ephesians 5:18-21—If a person is "filled" or becomes drunk with alcohol, how will it affect him?
  Drunkenness leads to debauchery (extreme indulgence in sensuality).

  If you are "filled" with the Holy Spirit, how will He affect your life?
  He will influence everything you do; Fruit of the Spirit, speak to one another with psalms, hymns and spiritual songs, sing and make music in your heart, always give thanks, submit to one another out of reverence to Christ.

LOOKING AT REAL LIFE:

	Indwelling of Holy Spirit	Filling of Holy Spirit
When	At salvation	At salvation
Frequency	Once, forever	Over and over, daily
Source	God does it automatically at salvation.	God does it as believer cooperates.
Conditions To Be Met	Initial faith of the believer	Daily submission of the believer

Look carefully at the Holy Spirit chart above. Discuss any questions or observations you may have.

4. What do you think is involved in submitting yourself to Christ daily (which is necessary in order to be filled with the Spirit)?

   Spending time with God, asking God to examine my life and show me any sin I'm not aware of, confessing any known sin, asking God to fill me with His Spirit, etc

LOOKING AT MY LIFE:

Which one of the Holy Spirit's ministries has been the most real to you lately and why?

_____ teaching you the truth

_____ convicting you of sin

_____ guiding you in the right direction

_____ making you more holy

_____ filling your life with His influence

_____ giving power to witness

_____ other_____

Spend some time alone with God right now, and talk with Him about submitting to Him, about being filled with His Spirit. Write a letter to Him or a prayer if that helps you focus and communicate with Him.

Leader: Lead the group through an exercise that will help group members deal with sin that may be preventing them from being filled with the Holy Spirit.
• Confess sin (I John 1:9).
• Submit life to Christ.
• Ask the Holy Spirit to fill my life.

Point out the two Exhibits to students: The Deity of the Holy Spirit and The Personality of the Holy Spirit that they can study on their own.

God's Righteousness

The phone call came late one night from a son in trouble. "Dad, I need some money!" After a brief discussion, I did what any Dad would do: I wire-transferred cash from my account to his. Later, he thanked me as we talked about the situation over a cup of coffee. We discussed how he got in the predicament (poor budgeting skills) and I helped him address those issues. He confessed that it was hard for him to admit that he needed help, but he was grateful nonetheless.

In a similar way it is hard for us to admit that we need God's help. But we too have failed. We have all sinned, fallen short of God's good, righteous requirements. What happened with my son and me illustrates in part what God has done for us. But instead of cash, He transfers righteousness to us. Then He comes alongside us in the Person of the Holy Spirit to help us continue to act righteously.

But what exactly is righteousness and how do we get it? Peter promised to follow Jesus to the death. Later he denied knowing Jesus and, when faced with the awful truth that he had abandoned Jesus in the time of testing, he wept bitterly (Matthew 26:31-35, 69-75).

It can be devastating to realize our weakness and inability to obey God. Words like "gratitude," "righteousness" and "faithfulness" can seem like oppressive reminders of our sins. But despite our failures to love and obey God, we can relate confidently to God because he makes us righteous.

> God is committed to bringing about righteousness in our lives.

Like Peter, we also continue to struggle with sin even after we have committed ourselves to follow Christ. And just as Peter learned, it is vital we understand that God will never abandon us. God is committed to bringing about righteousness in our lives. He does this in several stages.

INITIALLY, GOD DECLARES US RIGHTEOUS: JUSTIFICATION

[Note: The Exhibit, Sanctification Chart, on pg 77 will be useful to you as you read this Pocket Principle™. It shows when the 3 stages of salvation occur.]

Justification is a legal term that means we have been forgiven. In addition it means that we have been declared righteous—morally perfect (Romans 4:6-8). It is a "once-for-all-time" act that God accomplishes on our behalf. This does not mean we are habitually righteous in every thing we do, but it describes our legal standing with God. You can think of it as being given a new citizenship in God's Kingdom, a citizenship that cannot change no matter where you live. You may not have a passport to prove it, but God recognizes you as His and accepts you freely.

Being justified means that Christ's righteousness has been added to our "righteousness account" in the same way my money was transferred to my son's account. The result is that God now sees us as righteous on the basis of Jesus' perfect sacrifice. "God made Him who had no sin to be sin for us, so that in Him we might become the righteousness of God." (II Corinthians 5:21) The Apostle Paul describes this as a "right standing" with God that "is through faith in Christ—the righteousness that comes from God and is by faith." (Philippians 3:9)

This legal status before God is really a completely new relationship with Him. We are no longer enemies of God; we are now at peace with Him (Romans 5:1). In fact, we have immediate acceptance from God because sin is no longer a barrier between Him and His people. Romans 8:1 tells us, "there is now no condemnation for those who are in Christ Jesus." No matter what the circumstances, God will not abandon us nor revoke our status as being righteous.

PROGRESSIVELY, GOD MAKES US RIGHTEOUS: SANCTIFICATION

But what about our sins? What about the times when we, like Peter, turn away from God? Before Peter was tested, Jesus prayed that when Peter turned back to God, he would encourage his fellow believers. It is interesting to note that Jesus knew Peter would fall away, but He also expected Peter to return to Him and grow in righteousness.

Likewise, God has a plan for our lives that allows for the ups and downs in our lives and also includes our becoming holy or Christlike (II Corinthians 3:18). This process, called sanctification, begins when we are justified by God through faith in Christ and continues throughout our lives as we experience and grow in faith.

The Apostle Paul describes this sanctification process in his letter to the Philippian church:

Not that I have already obtained all this, or have already been made perfect, but I press on to take hold of that for which Christ Jesus took hold of me. Brothers, I do not consider myself yet to have taken hold of it. But one thing I do: Forgetting what is behind and straining toward what is ahead, I press on toward the goal to win the prize for which God has called me heavenward in Christ Jesus. (Philippians 3:12-14)

The process of sanctification involves pressing on, persevering in the heavenward path God has set us upon. Notice that sanctification is not only dependent on God, but on us as well. Paul also tells the Philippian believers they are to continue to "work out their salvation" even as God works in them (Philippians 2:12-13). Practically speaking, our sanctification involves our active participation with God, a lifelong perseverance to grow in Christlikeness.

Does this mean that by trying hard we can justify ourselves? By no means! Remember we are justified (declared "not-guilty") by trusting Christ. Paul explains: "For it is by grace you have been saved, through faith— and this not from yourselves, it is the gift of God—not by works, so that no one can boast." But he goes on to state, "For we are God's workmanship, created in Christ Jesus to do good works, which God prepared in advance for us to do." (Ephesians 2:8-10) God is the one who declares us righteous and He is the one who is at work in our lives to help us produce good works of righteousness. He has declared us righteous, legally. Then He helps us be righteous, actually. What an amazing God we follow!

FINALLY, GOD MAKES US PERFECTLY RIGHTEOUS: GLORIFICATION

God's work in our lives makes us citizens of His Kingdom and prepares us to be eternal residents of that Kingdom. One day, we will enter His Kingdom fully as citizens of heaven. To this end, we await the return of Christ, "who will transform our lowly bodies so that they will be like His glorious body." (Philippians 3:20-21)

> God is at work in us and will never abandon this good work He has begun!

When Jesus returns, we will experience the resurrection and be completely transformed to be like Him (except, of course, for His deity). In that day, God will glorify us, which is the completion of the good work of salvation that He began with our justification and continued with our sanctification (Philippians 1:6).

As you can see, the word "salvation" actually covers an amazing experience. Our salvation is rooted in a single, irreversible act of justification. It continues with our actively growing to become more what God wants us to be. One day this relationship will reach its full maturity when we are changed into morally perfect worshippers of God, forever.

Because of God's salvation, sin is no longer a barrier between God and us. We should not be discouraged when our growth in holiness is slow, because God is at work in us and will never abandon this good work He has begun. In confidence and security, we can always come to Him.

SUMMARY

We can relate confidently to God because He makes us righteous.

- God brings about righteousness in the believer's life in several stages.
- God declares us righteous, giving us immediate acceptance (justification).
- Sanctification is the process of becoming holy or Christlike.
- We must cooperate with God and persevere in our sanctification.
- Christ will return and complete what God has begun in us (glorification).

Sanctification Chart
Christlike Character

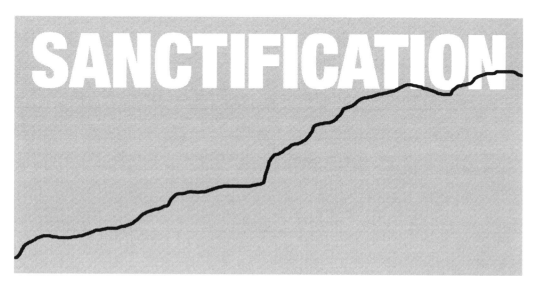

Justification
(Salvation)

Glorification
(Physical Death)

God's Righteousness

IMPORTANT to Leader: Answers and notes to leaders are in gray, italicized text.

GOAL:

For a disciple to understand God's righteousness and how it is applied to the believer's life.

GETTING STARTED:

Imagine you are in the midst of a long, arduous task. A task such as completing a PhD, a major house renovation, a multi-year project at work...What would help you stay healthy emotionally and mentally as you worked on this overwhelming project?

Breaking it into manageable parts instead of just concentrating on the whole; understanding the value of the project, the goal; the mutual help and encouragement of others, etc.

Transition: Because becoming like Christ is a long, "multi-year" project that isn't complete until we are in heaven with the Lord, God brings about righteousness in a believer's life in several stages.

Note: We refer to the Sanctification Chart *on page 77 throughout this lesson. It shows when the 3 stages of salvation occur.*

STUDYING TOGETHER & LOOKING AT REAL LIFE:

Stage 1 of Righteousness: Justification: Occurs at salvation; is a legal declaration whereby we are declared morally perfect (righteous).

Read Romans 3:21-24.

1. From this passage, describe how righteousness is applied to a believer's life.

   Righteousness is from God through faith (belief) in Christ, believer is justified freely by God's grace, no strings attached.

2. According to Romans 5:1, what is one result of our justification?

   Peace with God

3. What happens to a Christian if she forgets (or doesn't understand) that she is justified?

   Becomes legalistic, is under pressure to perform for God, is trying to gain acceptance by God, may be judgmental of others, etc.

Stage 2 of Righteousness: Sanctification: Is set apart for holy purposes.

Read II Corinthians 3:18.

4. What is the goal of sanctification?

   To be progressively (or ever-increasingly) transformed into Christ likeness

Read Hebrews 10:14.

5. This verse refers to 2 different aspects of sanctification. What are they?

   1. *By Jesus' sacrifice we have been made perfect forever (positional sanctification which takes place at salvation).*
   2. *And we are also being made holy (experiential sanctification which takes place throughout a believer's life).*

Read Philippians 2:12-13.

6. According to these verses, what roles do God and the believer play in the sanctification process?

   God works in the believer, the believer obeys and works out his salvation.

7. How did Paul work out his salvation (sanctification) with fear and trembling? (Read Philippians 3:12-14.)

   He was humble, continued pressing on (trusting God, stepping out in faith), didn't give up because of past failures, kept eternal values in sight

8. What are some unrealistic expectations Christians may have about the spiritual growth process?

   Spiritual growth is quick and easy, there shouldn't be struggles in the Christian life, "I have to be perfect or I'm a bad Christian," "If I just worked harder, I could sin less," "I'm the only person who struggles so much with sin," etc.

Stage 3 of Righteousness: Glorification: Occurs when God has made us like Him; when we are perfectly righteous.

Read I John 3:2-3; Philippians 1:6.

9. What is going to happen to the believer when Christ returns?

    God will carry on to completion the work He began (our sanctification); we shall be like His, perfectly pure

10. How does knowing that we will eventually be like Christ help a believer live the Christian life now?

    Motivates a believer to obey and follow God, encourages to endure difficulties, gives perspective in difficulties, gives hope

LOOKING AT MY LIFE:

As you look back over this lesson, what encouragement did God give you, and what concerns did it raise for you? How will you respond? Share with the group.

Leader: Ask the group to each pray about their own needs in sentence prayers.

Security In Christ

My daughter defines "friendship" as a relationship where "you can just be yourself." We all need relationships with people who love us and accept us completely, a place where we feel safe and secure. Every relationship is unique, but healthy relationships have this in common: they are based on trust, loyalty, and commitment. They are places where "we can just be ourselves."

An environment of honesty, goodwill, and unconditional love reassures us that we are relationally protected. When we are with people who love us in this way we are able to be transparent, which serves to deepen the relationship. We all need relationships with safe people who love us if we are to thrive and grow. This is also true in our relationship with God. If we feel loved and accepted by God we will approach Him in faith and with confidence. Conversely, if we feel condemned by God, we will not have a healthy relationship with Him. Being secure in our relationship with God requires two commitments. The first involves His eternal commitment to us, the second involves our commitment to stay in the relationship with Him.

GOD IS COMMITTED TO KEEPING US AS HIS CHILDREN.

Jesus spoke of His love for His followers by comparing Himself to a shepherd who walks in front of his flock, guarding them, leading them to good places, and reassuring them with his voice. "I give them eternal life," He said, "and they shall never perish; no one can snatch them out of my hand. My Father, who has given them to me, is greater than all; no one can snatch them out of my Father's hand. I and the Father are one." (John 10:27-30)

This remarkable assertion is founded on God's unswerving commitment to those whom He loves. Because of His unending love and unstoppable power, He is willing and able to guard us (II Timothy 1:12). Even sins and lack of faith will not lessen His commitment to those who are committed to Him. Timothy writes that, "if we are faithless, He will remain faithful, for He cannot disown Himself." (II Timothy 2:11-13) His love for us is not grounded upon our performance, it is grounded upon His perfect love and character.

> If we feel loved and accepted by God we will approach Him in faith and with confidence.

Make no mistake, God is holy and hates sin. But we still sin, even though we don't want to. When we do, we need to remember that God has made a way for us to be reconciled to Him. We have Someone who speaks to the Father in our defense—Jesus Christ, the Righteous One. He promises, "If we confess our sins, He is faithful and just and will forgive us our sins and purify us from all unrighteousness." (I John 1:8-2:2) Because Jesus Himself suffered temptations and yet did not sin, He is able to be the sacrifice for our sins and also to help us when we are tempted. Through Christ, God remains steadfast in His love to us.

WE ARE COMMITTED TO CONTINUE AS HIS CHILDREN.

Someone said that home is where they have to take you in when you knock on the door. Unfortunately, not all homes are so welcoming. But God always welcomes His children. And He wants us to be assured of our place in His family. Because we are His children, members of His family, we have a role also: our responsibility is to remain in His family.

John wrote his letter, the book of I John, so that people would know whether or not they were Christians. Central to his message was the confidence that Christians can have in their relationship with God. He writes: "I write these things to you who believe in the name of the Son of God so that you may know that you have eternal life." (I John 5:13) The confidence that He will never leave us causes us in turn to remain connected to Him, even when life is difficult.

> The confidence that He will never leave us causes us in turn to remain connected to Him, even when life is difficult.

John says, "I write these things" so you can have this assurance; so you can know for sure you are a believer. What are "these things" that he writes? He is referring to three evidences laid out in his letter that show a person that he has become a believer. These evidences are our love (4:7), our obedience (2:3-6) and our faith in Christ (4:15, 5:1a). It is not that we will demonstrate perfect love, obedience and faith but that we will experience each of these in ways we cannot explain apart from the fact that Christ is changing us on the inside. In these ways, the true believer remains faithful to the end, "if you continue in your faith, established and firm, not moved from the hope held out in the gospel." (Colossians 1:23)

At times we all face doubts, accusations, and even suffering. When this happens, it is essential to remember that we are God's children, committed to follow Him. The fact that we are God's children does not mean we never sin or disobey Him. Nor does it mean our salvation is dependent on our obedience. It does mean that we continually participate with God in our sanctification, working with Him by faith to grow in Christlikeness. As true believers we continue to, "work out [our] salvation with fear and trembling," because we love Him and trust Him, pressing on to fully gain the salvation that is already ours through Him (Philippians 2:12). To those who recognize both the divine and the human aspects of following the Living God, this approach is both mysterious and practical at the same time!

Put another way, God has given us everything we need to live a godly, holy life and be sure of our salvation. But we must make every effort to grow in righteousness, remembering that we have been cleansed from past sins and called to live as children of God. This way we confirm that God has brought us securely into His family.

His divine power has given us everything we need for life and godliness through our knowledge of Him who called us by His own glory and goodness. Through these He has given us His very great and precious promises, so that through them you may participate in the divine nature and escape the corruption in the world caused by evil desires.

For this very reason, make every effort to add to your faith goodness; and to goodness, knowledge; and to knowledge, self-control; and to self-control, perseverance; and to perseverance, godliness; and to godliness, brotherly kindness; and to brotherly kindness, love. For if you possess these qualities in increasing measure, they will keep you from being ineffective and unproductive in your knowledge of our Lord Jesus Christ. But if anyone does not have them, he is nearsighted and blind, and has forgotten that he has been cleansed from his past sins.

Therefore, my brothers, be all the more eager to make your calling and election sure. For if you do these things, you will never fall, and you will receive a rich welcome into the eternal Kingdom of our Lord and Savior Jesus Christ. (II Peter 1:3-11)

There is a basis for us to be secure in our relationship with God and be certain of our salvation. The basis of this security is God's eternal love coupled with His ability to keep us to the end. This is confirmed in our lives when we have a trusting dependence on Him and a maturing character.

SUMMARY

We can be secure in our relationship with God.

- A healthy relationship is based on trust, loyalty, and commitment.

- God is committed to keep us as His children.

- We can know we are God's children and be committed to Him.

- God has equipped us to live godly, holy lives, assured of our salvation.

Security In Christ

GOALS:

For a disciple to understand the basis for our security in Christ.
For a disciple to recognize evidences of salvation in himself.

GETTING STARTED:

How might insecurity in a relationship affect a person?

She may be fearful, hesitant, depressed, anxious, controlling, aggressive, etc.

How might insecurity affect the relationship?

Lack of trust, lack of honesty, no commitment, lack of loyalty, possessiveness, etc.

Transition: Insecurity in our relationship with God will affect that relationship in a similar way. Therefore, it is important that we as believers understand our security in Christ.

STUDYING TOGETHER:

Read John 10:22-29.

1. Who are the sheep?

    People who believe in Jesus, who listen to His voice, who follow Him

2. According to this passage, how secure are they?

    Security is guaranteed. Those who believe have eternal life; shall never perish, no one can snatch them out of God's hand.

Read John 6:37-40.

3. What are the arguments put forth here for the believer's security?

    Believers will not be rejected or lost. Jesus will never reject the people God has given to Him nor will He lose any of those given to Him.

4. Look again at the two John passages (John 10:22-29 and John 6:37-40). What do you think is the key concept that guarantees our security in Christ?

   God's character, His ability to keep us

Read I John 5:13.

5. What can we as believers know?

   That we have eternal life, that we are His children

In this book of I John, John mentions three evidences that we are God's children.

Read I John 2:3-6.   Read I John 4:7.   Read I John 4:15, 5:1a.

6. According to these passages what are three evidences that we know God and are His children?

   Obedience, love, faith (belief in Christ)

We have seen that a true believer can be sure of his salvation because of God's promises and because of evidences in his life. There is one more characteristic that shows that a person is a true believer.

Read Hebrews 3:14.

7. What does it mean to "come to share in Christ"?

   Become a believer; a Christian

   What additional characteristic of a true believer is listed in this verse?

   They hold firmly to their faith (confidence) to the end; they have enduring faith.

LOOKING AT REAL LIFE:

8. What are some of the reasons believers might feel insecure about their relationship with God?

   Concerned about the fact that they sin, have an overly sensitive conscience, struggle with having a devotional time, etc.

9. What are some helpful responses you can give to a person who feels insecure?

Address the specific reasons group members listed in #8 on previous page.

Important Note: There are four evidences that we are children of God presented in the Scriptures we read: obedience, love, faith and endurance. It is easy to have unrealistic expectations of ourselves in the Christian life. Sometimes evidences are small and may be overlooked. For example, we may be concerned that we are not being obedient or loving enough. However, the very fact we are concerned is evidence of a change! Someone who isn't a child of God is rarely concerned about a lack of love or lack of obedience.

LOOKING AT MY LIFE:

Christians aren't perfect; we don't live perfect lives. However, there should be some evidence of obedience, love, faith and endurance in our lives. What evidence (no matter how small) is there in your life that you are one of God's children?

Ask group members to give you feedback about evidences they see in your life that you are a believer.

Also, ask a good friend to share with you the changes he sees in your life.

Leader: Ask group members to pray prayers of thanksgiving for the evidences they see of God's work in their lives, and ask Him to continue His work.

What's Next?

We hope you enjoyed this study.
You may be wondering: "So, what's next?"
I'm glad you asked.

If your group has benefited from their experience with this study, we suggest that you continue the Cornerstone series. The next group of studies in this series is *Understanding People* (10 studies). The last group of studies in Cornerstone is *Growing Spiritually* (10 studies). All of these studies follow the same format as *Knowing God*. (See link on next page.)

Because you have chosen to lead, we want to do all we can to support you. In addition to the materials provided in this workbook, we would like to also offer you a free download of the Teaching Outlines for *Knowing God*.
(See link on next page.)

If you want to study materials that will help you grow as a leader, you might be interested in the *Small Groups Manual* (WDA) or the *Life Coaching Manual* (WDA), both can be found on the WDA store at www.disciplebuilding.org. (See link on next page.)

Also, **on the WDA website you will find explanations about the meaning of the different Phases I through V.** If you want to understand more about progressive growth there is a free download on our website called *Disciple Building: A Biblical Framework.* This explains the biblical basis for our disciple building process. (See links on next page.)

If you want to understand more about the Restorative Ministry, there is a free download entitled *How Emotional Problems Develop* on our website. The Restorative Ministry addresses relational and emotional needs that affect a disciple's ability to grow spiritually. (See links on next page.)

We look forward to a long association with you as you seek and follow our Lord, and grow in Christ using WDA Materials.

Bob Dukes

Links

Knowing God, Understanding People and *Growing Spiritually:*
www.disciplebuilding.org/product-category/laying-foundations-phase-2

Free Teaching Outlines for *Knowing God:*
http://www.disciplebuilding.org/materials/knowing-god-teaching-outlines-free-download

Small Groups Manual and *Life Coaching Manual:*
www.disciplebuilding.org/materials/description_materials/4
www.disciplebuilding.org/product-category/leadership-manuals

Meaning of Phases I-V:
www.disciplebuilding.org/about/phases-of-christian-growth/2

Free Download of *Disciple Building: A Biblical Framework:*
www.disciplebuilding.org/store/leadership-manuals/disciple-building-a-biblical-framework

Free Download of *How Emotional Problems Develop:*
www.disciplebuilding.org/store/leadership-manuals/how-emotional-problems-develop

About the Restorative Ministry:
www.disciplebuilding.org/ministries/restorative-ministry

About WDA

WDA's mission is to serve the church worldwide by developing Christlike character in people and equipping them to disciple others according to the pattern Jesus used to train His disciples.

Organized as Worldwide Discipleship Association (WDA) in 1974, we are based in the United States and have ministries and partners throughout the world. WDA is a 501c(3) non-profit organization funded primarily by the tax-deductible gifts of those who share our commitment to biblical disciple building.

WDA is committed to intentional, progressive discipleship. We offer a flexible, transferable approach that is based on the ministry and methods of Jesus, the Master Disciple Builder. By studying Jesus' ministry, WDA discovered five phases of Christian growth. This Cornerstone series focuses on the first and second phases, Phase I: Establishing Faith and Phase II: Laying Foundations (*Knowing God, Understanding People* and *Growing Spiritually*), which address the needs of a young believer or a more mature believer who wants a review of foundational Christian truths.

The remaining phases are: Phase III: Equipping for Ministry; Phase IV: Developing New Leaders and Phase V: Developing Mature Leaders.

For more information about WDA please visit our website: www.disciplebuilding.org.

If you are interested in seeing other WDA materials, please visit the WDA store: www.disciplebuilding.org/store.

WDA Partnerships

Help us build disciples worldwide.

You can help us fulfill the great commission by becoming a Worldwide Discipleship Association (WDA) partner. WDA's mission is to serve the church worldwide by developing Christlike character in people and equipping them to disciple others according to the pattern Jesus used to train His disciples.

Since our inception in 1974 our materials and processes have been used in more than 90 U.S. cities and in over **55 countries**. We have created **over a million direct discipleship impacts** and have conducted face-to-face **training to over 17,000 pastors and leaders** around the globe! **Your support of WDA is vital to the success of our mission.** We pledge to serve as faithful stewards of your generous gifts to the ministry.

www.disciplebuilding.org/give/wda-partnership

Become a Partner Today

44723510R00058

Made in the USA
San Bernardino, CA
21 January 2017